We would like to dedicate this work to Akshay Ashok, Jay Sharma and Shirin Suri, for being constantly there for us, through thick and thin, during our work on this book.

REGULATION AND RESOLUTION IN THE PULLULATING INDIAN COMMERCIAL SECTOR

CHECK ON STATUTORY SUFFICIENCY

VAISHNAVI SALIMATH AND TEJAS SATEESHA HINDER

Made with ♥ on the Notion Press Platform
www.notionpress.com

Contents

Foreword

The rapidly growing Indian commercial sector brings with it, multiple challenges for regulation and dispute resolution due to the delay in statutory upgradation alongside the respective developments, as well as absence of foresight over feasbility in legal regulation post such developments and obliviousness to prospective nature of disputes that could arise.

This book covers five such developments in the commercial field, which call for strict statutory revamp due to the insufficiency of the same in the status quo, and indicates how these developments could be accommodated statutorily.

Preface

Due to the slow pace of statutory revision alongside the corresponding developments, the absence of foresight regarding the viability of legal regulation following such developments, and ignorance regarding the potential nature of disputes that may arise, the rapidly expanding Indian commercial sector poses numerous challenges for regulation and dispute resolution.

This book covers a wide range of developments, ranging from the very recent Special Purpose Acquisition Companies to arbitrability of corporate disputes, and lays down prospective means to regulate the same and dismiss any loopholes that could prospectively arise in the process.

Acknowledgements

We would like to thank the National Law Institute University, Bhopal for supporting us with the online and libarary infrastructure that helped us complete this work.

CHAPTER ONE

INTERNATIONAL COMMERCIAL ARBITRATIONS WITH SEAT IN INDIA: ADVANTAGES, CHALLENGES AND THE ROAD AHEAD

Background

With the rise in commercial activities and globalisation, the world has transformed into a predominant multicultural hub. Corporate entities have expanded beyond borders and cross-border transfers have also risen in real time. Agreements and agreements between private entities are always ugly, thereby giving rise to conflicts that are not under the boundaries of a single country's municipal regulation, since contracts are 'cross-border' in nature.

Arbitration is a preferred method for the resolution of disputes chosen by the parties in which the parties intentionally opt to refer their case to a neutral third party and choose to be bound by its verdict. There has been a huge spike in foreign firms working out of India in recent years. This has resulted in a rise in the number of international arbitrations with its arbitration seat in India.

This part through a doctrinal research and methodological triangulation attempts to study the status quo of the Indian Legal Position with respect to International Commercial Arbitration, through an expansive study of the Arbitration and Conciliation Act, 1996 (hereinafter "the Act), the 2015 and 2019 Amendments to the Act along with other related legislations, and judicial precedents, which have contributed towards development of the surrounding jurisprudence. This part critically analyses the existing position in relation to such arbitrations seated in India, by looking into the nature of awards rendered and their enforceability, the position of arbitrators after the recent legislative and judicial developments and parties as stakeholders.

Introduction

The adjudication of cross-border business disputes involves knowledge of a different nature, particularly because the entities in dispute come from countries which have different legal structures, such as the common law system and the civil law system. Typically, as a matter of procedure, all agreements performed between firms inter-se, have three agreements, worth stressing, in particular, to put to fruition a shared purpose; the first of which is that of the governing statute, the second is the jurisdiction clause and the third is the 'arbitration clause'. The 'governing statute' stipulation specifies that, if and when agreements between multinational companies go bad, the law of which country will be used. As long as the courts in which country have a say in the matter of question are concerned, the jurisdiction clause says. The 'arbitration clause' specifies how the issues between the companies must be settled before they are officially taken before the court of law for adjudication; the arbitration clause talks to procedures such as mediation, conciliation and arbitration that are of the context of' out-of-the-court-settlement-of-disputes.'

The international community has held a close eye on the development of arbitration laws in India due to some contentious decisions taken by the Indian judiciary in the last two decades, especially in cases involving a foreign party. For its intervention in international arbitrations and extra-territorial enforcement of domestic rules in foreign arbitrations, the Indian judiciary has also been attacked. However, by recent court rulings, the new trends in arbitration jurisprudence clearly represent the assistance of the judiciary in allowing India to follow the best international practises. A pro-arbitration policy has been introduced by the judiciary, and pro-arbitration decisions by the Supreme Court of India and the High Courts have attempted to fully reform India's arbitration environment.

To guarantee the absence of actual and anticipatory prejudice, more often than not, parties engaged in international commercial transactions select the 'seat' of arbitration in a country that has little to do with the business transactions of the participating organisations. Commercial transactions executed between the parties typically allow for the institutional code of ethics for arbitration to be valid. The substantive law that rules the conflict relating to the agreement in question is most commonly indicated and assertively decided by the parties.

Legislative and Judicial Background

In India, arbitration law is regulated by the 1996 Arbitration and Conciliation Act. The 1996 Act is based on the Model Law of UNCITRAL. Broadly speaking, the 1996 Act is split into two sections:' Part I' and 'Part II'. Domestic arbitration is protected by Part I of the 1996 Statute, while International Commercial Arbitration is covered by Part II.

Section 2(1)(f) of the Act defines 'international commercial arbitration' as an arbitration relating to disputes arising out of legal relationships, whether contractual or not, considered as commercial under the law in force in India and where at least one of the parties is— (i) an individual who is a national of, or habitually resident in, any country other than India; or (ii) a body corporate which is incorporated in any country other than India; or (iii) an association or a body of individuals whose central management and control is exercised in any country other than India; or (iv) the Government of a foreign country.

Consistency with Model Law establishes this concept. Article 1(3) applies the principle of internationality which includes situations in which the place of settlement, the place of execution of the contract or the place of the subject-matter of the litigation are located outside the State in which the parties have a place of operation, or cases where the sides have expressly decided that more than one country applies to the subject-matter of the arbitration arrangement. UNCITRAL emphasises on the location of companies, while the 1996 Act focuses on nationality.[1] A definition of the word 'commercial' is absent in the Act. In the UNCITRAL Model Law on International Commercial

Arbitration, however, this concept finds clarification and because the Model Law finds reference in the Preamble annexed to the 1996 Act, the same can very well be used for guidance. The Supreme Court of India, in the case of R.M. Investment & Trading Co. (P) Ltd. v. Boeing Co.[2], held that, as far as the legislation relating to arbitration is concerned, the term 'economic' should be understood as narrowly as possible.

An explicit review of Part II of the Act notes brings to light that international commercial arbitration shall subsist except if the seat of arbitration is in India. In the case of Bharat Aluminium Co. v. Kaiser Aluminium Technical Services Inc.[3] (hereinafter "BALCO"), setting to rest all legal speculations, the Supreme Court of India ruled that, where the seat of arbitration in international commercial arbitration is outside India, Section I of the Act is not valid. The Supreme Court of India ruled in the case of Bhatia International v. Bulk Trading SA[4] that Section I of the 1996 Act was applicable also to the International Commercial Arbitrations with their 'seat' outside the jurisdiction of India. Thus, the BALCO case significantly overruled the Bhatia case. As regards the applicability of Section I of the 1996 Act to International Commercial Arbitrations, the rule laid down by the Bhatia case was overturned, prospectively, by the BALCO case. Therefore, the Bhatia case also holds the ground and prospectively applies with regard to arrangements entered into by the parties before 06.09.2012, that is, the date on which the BALCO case judgement was made. The effect is therefore that, in the case of BALCO, the ratio is not applicable to a large number of cases in which the parties entered into an international commercial transaction prior to 06.09.2012, but the disputes arose after 06.09.2012.

The effectiveness of the International Commercial Arbitration, which the Supreme Court of India sought to infuse into the arbitral mechanism through its judgement in the BALCO case, remains a subject of contentious criticism.

The Supreme Court of India, giving primacy to intention of parties in designation of a seat, has held that the intention of a party designating an arbitration seat to confer exclusive jurisdiction on the courts having jurisdiction to supervise the seat. Furthermore, unless there is an intention to the contrary, the place of arbitration designated in the arbitration clause, whether described by the nomenclature of the seat or venue or place, shall be the legal seat of arbitration.

Furthermore, the narrative in the Indian legal system is that of implied inclusion when it comes to exclusion from Indian laws. In a critical case, the Supreme Court of India, Harmony Innovation Shipping Ltd. v. Gupta Coal India Ltd.[5], addressed the anomaly of the implied exclusion of Indian laws under an arbitration agreement. The court, emphasising on the contractual history, the context of the contract, and the circumstances of the parties qua which the parties acted and the background qua which the communication was made, held that it was not possible to refuse the relevant law solely because it would place one of the parties in an advantageous position.

Much like other jurisdictions, India has also been faced with the 'Seat v. Venue' debate, which the judiciary substantively resolved in the Enercon case[6], in which it was held that the 'place' of an arbitration, which is the geographical location chosen on the basis of the convenience of the parties, is not the same as the 'place' of the arbitration, which defines the proper jurisdiction, and that it is an agreed proposal of law that the 'legal seat' or 'place of arbitration' typically brings with it the option of the curial law of the respective country. Making the position clearer, the Court went on to state that:

i. It is necessary not to confuse the legal seat of arbitration with the geographically convenient place or places for holding hearings;
ii. If the "seat" of arbitration is in India; the 1996 Act being the curial law, recourse to Indian Courts as per Part I of the 1996 Act, including Section 9 thereof is available to the parties. The "seat" of arbitration thus, would be the country whose law is chosen as the curial law by the parties;
iii. An arbitration agreement is valid so far as the intention of the parties to resolve the dispute by arbitration is clear; any allegation of non-conclusiveness of the main contract is immaterial;
iv. If the intention to arbitrate is clear, the court can make good an omission to make the arbitration agreement workable.

The courts of the 'seat' of arbitration have, therefore, sole authority over the arbitration process to exercise supervisory powers. In this respect, the courts of the 'place' of arbitration cannot have simultaneous jurisdiction.

Referral to arbitration under Part II of the Act

Under Section 45 of the Act, a judicial authority has been allowed to refer all parties to arbitration who have entered into an arbitration agreement under Section 44 of the Act. It is founded on Article II(3) of the Convention and it can be clearly understood, as read in Section 45 of the Act, that it is necessary for the judicial authority to refer the parties to an arbitration proceeding.

Section 45 of the Act begins with a non-obstante clause, giving the rule an overarching effect and making it prevail over all that is contradictory to that found in Part I of the Act or the Code of Civil Procedure of India. It grants the Indian judicial authority the right to strictly execute the arrangement of arbitration between the parties. But the court must be assured that the arrangement is legitimate, operative and capable of being enforced as a necessary pre-condition for specifically implementing the arbitration agreement. In the absence of a review by the court to determine the legality of the arbitration arrangement, a claimant will not be entitled to a stay of judicial proceedings instituted in contravention of the arbitration agreement referred to in Section 45. The analysis should be done on a prima facie basis.[7]

With respect to the threshold of jurisdiction given to the judiciary, Section 8 and Section 45 of the Act, both relating to the court sending cases to arbitration, differ. The main difference seems to be that in the case of sending parties to arbitration, Section 8 of the Act leaves no discretion to the judge, while Section 45 allows the court the right to deny a referral to arbitration if it determines that the arbitration arrangement is null and void, inoperative or incapable of being carried out.

However, the Supreme Court has ruled that, contrary to Section 45 of the Act, no specific filing is required to petition a court to refer the issue to arbitration. If a party so asks, even where an affidavit is made, the court is obliged to refer the matter to arbitration, with the single exception in situations where the arbitration arrangement is null and invalid, inoperative or incapable of being enforced, thus restricting the extent of judicial review at the point of referral to international arbitrations.

Thus, while Section 8 of the Act allows for an application to be submitted by a party to the suit requesting a reference to arbitration in the case, Section 45 includes only a 'motion' for that reason. Furthermore, Section 45 may be extended only when the case is the subject of an arbitration arrangement of the New York Convention, while Section 8 usually extends to all arbitration provisions coming under Part I of the Act. Thus, even non-signatory parties will pray and be sent to arbitration on any of the agreements, the principle notably brought out in the case of Chloro Controls[8].

This decision has widespread consequences for international owners and groups, as also non-parties such as parent firms, branches, group companies or directors can be referred to and made parties to the arbitration in certain exceptional situations including hybrid transactions and interlinked agreements.

Ad Hoc Arbitration in India and Indian Arbitration Institutions

For various factors, the existence of ad hoc arbitration has been viewed as a significant roadblock to modernisation and change. In an ad hoc environment, organisations have a variety of distinct benefits that are missed.[9] First, they are better equipped to handle cases, control fees and costs, police conflicts of interest, and hold arbitrators liable for misconduct by providing an administrative buffer between neutrals and end-users. Second, the vast majority of ad hoc arbitrators are former judges who may be ill-equipped to serve parties who wish to realise the benefits traditionally attributed to arbitration, accustomed to the technical rules of procedure and the slow pace of litigation in India. Third, on a per sitting basis, ad hoc arbitrators usually fee, which facilitates liberal adjournments and a tradition of conducting frequent brief meetings instead of reserving blocks of day-long sessions.[10] As a result, expenditures will spin out of control easily.[11]

There are examples of cases in which the arbitrators‘ remuneration (not counting charges and lawyers' fees) alone exceeds the amount in question. Retired judges charge anywhere from Rs. 10 million (about US $ 1,500) to Rs. 50 million (about US $ 7,500) a day, minus expenses, by one estimate.[12] It is not unusual for such costs to require first class flights and trials in five-star hotels in high-stakes situations. Institutions, by comparison, usually place restrictions on the remuneration and operating expenses of arbitrators and offer hearing services at a modest pace. Calls for structural reform have gradually pointed to these and other shortcomings of the ad hoc method.

While India's institutional arbitration market remains miniscule, there seems to be no lack of provider institutions, some of which are private and others associated with the High Courts. The Indian Council on Arbitration, which has been in operation for five decades, is one of the largest and most commonly used private providers. Others include the FCCI Arbitration and Conciliation Tribunal (FACT) established in 1952, the Nani Palkhivala Arbitration Centre established in 2005, and the Indian Merchants Chamber Suresh Kotak International Arbitration Centre established in 2014. Arbitral institutions affiliated with High Courts include the Delhi International Arbitration Centre (DAC) established in 2009 and the Arbitration and Conciliation Centre, Bengaluru established in 2012.

Currently, there is no centralised law in India governing arbitral agencies. Provider institutions are also self-regulating as a result. Many have a regulatory authority, have enacted their own laws of arbitration, and hold a tribunal of arbitrators. Typical prerequisites for entry to a tribunal are a minimum of 15 years of legal experience and, unlike practise at existing international organisations such as the London Court of International Arbitration (LCIA) or the Singapore International Arbitration Centre (SIAC), parties are generally not able to appoint arbitrators from outside the panel. Importantly, arbitral agencies often publish compensation schedules which restrict the payments of arbitrators according to the value of the argument or counterclaim, thereby facilitating accountability and minimising adjournment and delay rewards.

Arbitral Awards: Enforceability and Costs

Enforceability: An understanding of the position surrounding Domestic and Foreign Awards

Contrary to the assumption that after the award is announced, an arbitral suit will cease, the substantive lawsuit continues when the award is to be enacted following the presentation. The lawmakers choose to make arbitral awards open to appeal before the circuit courts, for reasons better known to them. The awards given by a jury of three former Chief Justices of the Supreme Court are subject to the review of a trial judge. Instead, the arbitration experience will prove to be frustrating, lengthy and lopsided, conveniently negating the notion of swift and meaningful justice, particularly for the successful claimant. We can only imagine the plight of a good claimant who, before those legal challenges come to an end, can not celebrate the arbitral prize.

When a party requires compliance of a New York Convention award according to the rules of the Act, with an original/duly authenticated copy of the award, an original/ duly authenticated copy of the arrangement, and proof sufficient to show that the award is an international award, it must make an appeal to the Court of competent jurisdiction.

Enlisted below are the pre-requisites for successful enforcement of foreign awards of international commercial arbitrations:

- Existence of a commercial transaction: In order to settle contractual conflicts resulting from a legal arrangement, the award must be granted in the convention country. The Supreme Court noted in the case of RM Investment & Trading v. Boeing[13] that the word 'economic' can be commonly understood as having access to several practises that are an important part of foreign trade.
- Existence of a Written Agreement: The Geneva Convention and the New York Convention specify that, while it does not have to be formally worded or in line with a standard format, an international arbitral agreement needs to be made in writing.
- Valid and Enforceable Agreement: The foreign award must be legitimate and result from a commercial arrangement which is enforceable. The Supreme Court ruled in the case of Khardah Corporation v. Raymon & Co.[14] that an arbitration provision cannot be applied if it is deemed unconstitutional by the arrangement of which it forms an integral part. In order to make the arbitration arrangement effective and binding on the parties, it a settled legal position in the Indian Jurisprudence that a document involving an arbitration

agreement must be signed by all parties to the contract.[15]

- Clarity of Award: The Supreme Court held in the case of Koch Navigation v. Hindustan Petroleum Corp.[16] that the courts shall give force to an award which, under Indian law, is simple, unambiguous and capable of resolution.

As a result of several judicial interpretations of some seminal decisions such as Bhatia International v. Bulk Trading[17], Venture Global Engineering v. Satyam Machine Ltd.[18] and Bharat Aluminum Co v. Kaiser Aluminum Technical Service[19], the thin line of difference between a foreign and domestic arbitral award was drawn. The court in Bharat Aluminum observed that Part I of the act exclusively lays down the procedures and guidelines for domestic arbitrations whereas Part II of the act in accord with the UNCITRAL Model Law, New York Convention and Geneva Convention applies to foreign seated arbitrations. It should be noted that arbitrations under Part I include both, arbitration in India between two Indian parties and international commercial arbitration held in India. Under the processes referred to in Section II of the Act, International Commercial Arbitrations conducted outside India will be controlled. Under the processes referred to in Section II of the Act, International Commercial Arbitrations conducted outside India will be controlled. Excessive interference by the court in the form of judicial review has hindered the process of dispute settlement and frustrated the intent of the act. The act alluded to in Section 34 sets out a list of grounds for moving an appeal to the court appealing the arbitral award. Article 34 of the UNCITRAL Model Law 1985 specifies that

Section 34 of the Act is a brain child and its scope in the 1996 Act is even broader than the repealed 1940 Act. Section 34(2)(A) applies to five sub-provisions in which a party is expected to furnish concrete facts to the court to set aside the arbitral award in respect of the appeal.

Firstly, if the subject-matter of the case is not worthy of arbitration resolution in India, and secondly, if the award is contrary to the 'Public Policy of India.' The Supreme Court viewed 'economic policy' in the sense of the concepts governing the 1996 Statute, the Indian Contract Act, 1872 and the Statutory clauses in ONGC v. Saw Pipes Ltd.[20] By improving the likelihood of a near unlimited judicial appeal, Saw Pipes broadened the reach of public regulation, defeating the goal of limited court intervention of the Act. Therefore, the decision of Saw Pipes is a major blemish on the arbitration jurisprudence of India.

Cost & Time: An examination of their mutual contingency

The costs are awarded not as a penalty to the defeated party or as a bonus to the party receiving them, but as a reward to the successful party in order to compensate him for legal expenses, although not entirely, to which he has been subjected in the prosecution of his lawsuit or his defense.[21] The scope of arbitration costs has become broader in the last few years. Arbitration costs now include the fee payable to the arbitrators for 'reading fees',' sitting fees',' award writing fees' and other expenses, combined with the costs of arranging sessions (often at luxury hotels), parties, witnesses, counsel and arbitrator travel charges.

The overall expense can sometimes run into crores that are outrageous for a developing country like India. It is thought that the lack of ad-valorem court fees payable on an arbitral claim makes the process affordable and convenient.[22] The parties are under the impression that by paying for the arbitrator's fee, counsel fee, administrative costs and stamp duty on arbitral award, the court fee is saved but end up paying more or less the same amount. No doubt the costs could (and should) be taken into account in the award to be passed, but the fact remains that the arbitral proceedings are costly by any standards and not inexpensive. The court also observed that it is necessary to find an urgent solution for the problem to save arbitration from the arbitration costs and opined that 'Institutional Arbitration' has come close to providing a solution.

It must be noted that only when the number of arbitration proceedings is limited does the arbitration process prove cost-effective. However, as arbitration becomes litigation in disguise, the delays caused by judicial intervention drain the finances of the parties. Ironically, speed and cost effectiveness are hallmarks of the procedure and the reasons why arbitration is preferred to litigation, particularly in commercial disputes, as a viable option for dispute resolution. A hurdle to be overcome is to make India's arbitration friendly destination cost-effective.

As per the recommendations of the 246th Law Commission Report the legislature has added Section 31(A) to the Act. It empowers the Court or Arbitral Tribunal to have discretion to determine whether costs are payable by one party to another, amount of such costs, and when such costs are to be paid. The Fourth Schedule has also been added to the Act, which establishes a fixed model fee depending on the amount in dispute and the percentage share based on the amount of the claim. It also provides that an additional amount of 25% of the fee payable (as per the 'Fourth Schedule' provisions) will be added where only a single arbitrator is an arbitral tribunal.

The model fee refers to arbitration as well as arbitrations where parties have agreed to set fees in accordance with the arbitral institution's rules under which arbitral proceedings are to be conducted. These deficiencies are capable of hampering the progress of international trade and trade arbitration. Strengthening international arbitration and providing for a more cost-effective and time-saving process that is more stable can help India attract foreign investors and commercial entities, which is the government's objective.

Non-enforcement of arbitral awards: Understanding the grounds

Under Section 48 of the Act, an Indian court may refuse to impose an international arbitral award in the case of a New York Convention award, whether it falls beyond the limits of the following statutory defences.

i. The parties to the agreement are under some incapacity;
ii. The agreement is void;
iii. The award contains decisions on matters beyond the scope of the arbitration agreement;
iv. The composition of the arbitral authority or the arbitral procedure was not in accordance with the arbitration agreement;
v. The award has been set aside or suspended by a competent authority of the country in which it was made;
vi. The subject matter of dispute cannot be settled by arbitration under Indian law; or
vii. The enforcement of the award would be contrary to Indian public policy. The term "public policy", as mentioned under Section 48(2)(b), is one of the

conditions to be satisfied before enforcing a foreign award.

It is a settled position in the Indian jurisprudence that the enforcement of an international award must be denied on the basis that, if such enforcement were contrary to India's fundamental policy, the interest of India or justice or morals, it was contrary to public policy.[23]

A foreign award shall be considered to be a decree of the Indian court administering the award, in accordance with the constitutional requirements alluded to above, which shall consequently be binding on the parties entitled to the award for all purposes. The Supreme Court has ruled that no special application for the award to be executed needs to be filed. A two-stage process will be subject to a single application for the compliance of the award. The enforceability of the award will be calculated in the first process, taking into account the provisions of the Act (New York Convention grounds). If legitimate, international arbitration awards are considered at the same degree as a decision passed by an Indian civil court and are enforceable by Indian courts having jurisdiction as if those courts had passed the decree.

In fact, the 2015 Amendment Act offers an interpretation of Section 48 of the Act to avoid any uncertainty that an award is in conflict with India's public policy. Only if I the award was induced or affected by fraud or corruption or in breach of Section 75 or Section 81; or (ii) in breach of the basic policy of Indian law; or (iii) conflicts with the most fundamental concepts of morality or justice.

Public Policy: What and How?

A term often left open ended without an exhaustive definition under enforceability is Public Policy. An explanation that briefly clarifies what is to be understood in India's public policy next to Section 34(2)(b) involves fraud, corruption and violation of Section 75 or Section 81, but does not serve its purpose. Since the term 'public policy' has not been provided with a definitive meaning under the 1996 Act or any other statute, the scope of this expression has gradually increased over the years through judicial craftsmanship, giving vast discretion to the courts to interpret it accordingly. This has recently caused a lot of difficulties for litigants in international commercial arbitration and investment arbitration, as the courts have whimsically rejected and accepted claims on this ground. However, the 2015 Amendment Act clarifies that an award will not be set aside by the court merely by misapplication of the law or by re-appreciation of evidence. In deciding whether the award is in contravention of the basic policy of Indian law, the court will not review the merits of the dispute. The question to be answered after the Saw Pipes judgement is precisely what the court meant by the term 'Patent Illegality'. In the context of arbitration, one can infer multiple meanings of the word 'illegality'. One can infer multiple meanings of the word 'illegality' in the arbitration context. The unlawful existence of the underlying deal, the object of the contract or the circumstances involving the arbitration arrangement are some ideas, but in the Saw Pipes judgement, the Supreme Court gave the term 'illegality' a whole new dimension by equating it to 'error of law.' Upon that observation, one can deduce that if the courts are granted the right to review on the basis of inconsistency of law, then the purpose of the Act is immediately undermined and settlement is the beginning of successive appeals to the highest court of the country, rendering it no different from litigation.

That is the same as maintaining the grounds for appeal under Section 30 of the 1940 Act that were still open. Moreover, a close review of the 1996 Act reveals that, contrary to the explicit terms of the contract or substantive legislation, the two requirements for setting aside the award are now arguably available under Sections 34(2)(a)(iv) and 34(2)(a)(v) respectively. A three-month time limit has been defined under Section 34(3), during which an attempt to set aside an arbitral award must be made. The time frame began on the day on which the order was issued by the claimant. A further extension of thirty days can be extended to the petitioner in the event that it can present substantial evidence that it has been hindered by a legitimate excuse for the claim to be submitted within three months. There is a need to rethink the latter method. The Act was framed for the litigants to be easily and efficiently redressed, but in doing so, one could not lose sight of opportunities that should discourage an honest litigant from pursuing his right to be heard. Those people are prohibited from pursuing relief by the terms of Section 34(3). The privileges granted by substantive legislation do not interfere with procedural law. The objective of the act should certainly be of utmost significance, but the objective of ensuring justice should not be overlooked when doing so. Therefore, the terms of the act include formulation in a way that preserves our legal system's objectives and ideals.

Two tier and appellate Arbitrations in view of the Indian Legal Position

The objective of the Act was to provide for an integral unified framework and envisages only one arbitrator, as reflected in multiple judgments.[24] The Act envisages only one award under one set of rules, not multi-layer awards governed by different sets of rules.[25] By reason of Section 36 of the 1996 Act[26], a specified time period is being granted for setting aside an award unless it becomes executed and enforced. It does not envision a situation of appeal to different forum post that period to set aside the award.[27] The Doctrine of Merger[28] too won't apply in the present case, because if the appellate arbitration is allowed, the second award would lose its character of an award given it is post the enforcement of first award.[29] Hence, this case cannot be claimed as a mixture of both two types of proceedings as they are not in continuation but different in structure.[30] An appeal if not filed within the time limit, the arbitrator would have no injunction to stay the operation of the original award.[31] Under Section 34 of the Act[32], it is clearly laid down that " The Courts ..." giving the impression that only courts under national jurisdiction has the ability to set aside the award, not any other body vested power by the parties.[33] If during the pendency of the alleged appeal the award becomes a decree, it won't be of any use.

Agreements allowing for two-tier arbitrations would be in violation of the principles of finality and the balance of judicial intervention as envisioned in the Act. This is clearly reflected by the words 'final and binding' as used under Section 35 of the Statute. Further, under Indian Jurisprudence, the party autonomy has always did yield to judicial intervention.[34] A fortiori, the validity of a domestic award cannot be questioned before any other forum including the forum chosen by the parties, if any.[35] A lack of explicit impressibility in the statute may be contended. But the same can be refuted on the basis that the silence of a particular provision doesn't entail its presence[36] if there are other restricting implicit factors present i.e. public policy in the given case.

The term 'arbitration agreement' under Section 7 doesn't envision two different awards in a particular agreement, as awards are 'final and binding'.[37] Also, it has been held that an appeal can sustain only within a submission subject to a same set of rules, not different procedures.[38]

There are many well settled benefits of International Commercial Arbitration that tend to get eroded if appellate arbitration is allowed for.[39] This can be that of finality[40] one of the prime concerns of arbitral proceedings.[41] It mostly renders inefficient primary awards, is time-consuming and costly and acts against the interest of the weaker party.[42] This is why many global jurisdictions like that of UK and India have despised this and opted to stay away from this.[43] One of the primary objectives of the 1996 Act was to avoid unnecessary delay and expenses[44], which would stand defeated if appellate arbitration is allowed.

A common or separate legislation for domestic and international arbitration: Constructs and Narratives

International commercial arbitration is gaining momentum. Although there are various opinions, the Arbitration and Conciliation Act, 1996, has largely succeeded in enforcing foreign awards effectively in India. Many disputes that end in arbitration lend themselves to a variety of advantage strategies for lawyers, often involving a variety of opportunities to gain advantage, often involving a variety of opportunities to delay, disrupt and frustrate the process. Unfortunately, India's litigation system is not a credible way to achieve a fair, timely, affordable and (most significantly, perhaps) enforceable outcome. The problems of the Indian justice system are well documented: experience shows that other key locations share similar, if not worse, problems. Apart from the usual disadvantages of using certain courts (namely delay, cost, advertising, incompetence, bias, corruption, etc.), the primary issue remains that of our country's courts. It is advisable to have proper ADR provisions in all contracts, considering the Indian scenario, particularly delays in courts. The overriding canon in determining the place of arbitration is the degree of judicial interventionism in the arbitral process.

As a general proposition, the ruling of an arbitrator is virtually unreviewable on merits for all practical purposes. 30 Disregarding this cardinal principal would make enforcement of arbitral awards difficult, the grey areas in enforcement of arbitration awards should be removed as India is going to become the center of international arbitration, booming in the economy geographically and strategically. International commercial arbitration, however, is on a separate footing where it appoints knowledgeable, diligent and equitable arbitrators from both the legal and corporate communities. In the international domain and a constricted one in the domestic sphere, the Indian Courts should support a constitutional view.

Emerging Issues: An overlook through the 2019 Amendment Act and the 2021 Bill

It is important to flag out that the Act was substantially overhauled without the 2019 reform before we dive through all other judicial developments or reviews. A number of sections have been notified, and a number of essential clauses, such as the creation of the Arbitration Council of India, have yet to be notified. The most significant notified provisions of the 2019 Amendment Act, in so far as they pertain to international commercial arbitrations are as follows:

- **Revised timeline for the submission of pleadings:** Section 23 of the Statute, which deals with the filing of pleadings by the parties to an arbitration, has been amended to include a clear timeframe, i.e. a declaration of argument must be submitted by the complainant and a statement of defence must be filed by the respondent within 6 months of the date of notice of the appointment of the arbitral tribunal.
- **Revised timeline for passing of an arbitral award:** Before the 2019 reform, arbitral tribunals were required within 12 months of the date on which the tribunal was named to deliver the arbitral award. This timetable has been expanded so that, with the possibility of a 6-month extension, the clock begins ticking from the date from which the parties' pleadings are finished. However, this timeframe is not valid in the case of an international commercial arbitration, and the arbitral tribunal only has to make an attempt to stick to it. Therefore, this procedural provision has been eased by the 2019 Reform, which is presumably in view of the greater scope of the problems and pleadings therein, and a related improvement in the difficulty of the mandate of a tribunal.
- **Confidentiality and Protection of Arbitrators:** As inserted by the 2019 Amendment Act, Sections 42A and 42B of the Act provide for the secrecy of arbitration proceedings / the subsequent arbitral award for all arbitrations and for the protection of arbitrators from suits and proceedings for actions and omissions they have performed in the course of arbitration

proceedings. In the global arbitration culture, these concerns have already been a challenge and the codification of these protections by India is one further step towards the goal of aligning India's arbitration system with best practices that are internationally agreed.

- **Applicability of the 2015 Amendment Act:** The newly inserted Section 87 of the Act clarified in an attempt to put an end to the debate on the retrospective applicability of the 2015 Amendment Act that the 2015 Amendment Act would only apply to it: (a) arbitrations proceedings which commenced after the date of notification of the 2015 Amendment; and (b) court proceedings in relation to arbitrations which commenced following the 2015 Amendment Act, and not court proceedings which were in relation to pre-Amendment arbitration proceedings, but which were themselves commenced after the 2015 Amendment Act. This caused a major hue and cry in the legal community with respect to various issues.

While the aim of the 2019 Amendment Act is to provide certification to arbitral institutions and arbitrators by grading and accrediting the Arbitration Council of India, the constitution of the Arbitration Council of India itself is largely governed by government, which may threaten the independence of arbitration in India. It must be noted, however, that provisions relating to the Arbitration Council of India have not yet been notified in the 2019 Amendment Act. The 2019 Amendment Act may also have missed the opportunity to make appropriate exceptions to the confidentiality obligation.

The insufficiency of special cases for the confidentiality commitment may offer ascent to different issues. For example, the accompanying conditions would require revelation and would not carefully fall inside the extent of the special case proposed in the 2019 Amendment Act, which would involve situations where:

1. Where a party files for an anti-arbitration injunction before the civil court;
2. Where a party approaches a government regulator on facts which also gives rise to a contractual dispute;
3. Where information is proposed to be shared with third party experts (such as forensic, accounting, delay or quantum experts); or
4. Where information is required to be shared with a third-party funder to obtain funding for a claim.

The 2021 Bill gets rid of the previously mentioned issues identifying with arrangement to a huge degree, by getting rid of the qualifications of the arbitrators under the Eighth Schedule of the Arbitration and Conciliation Act, 1996 which determined that the judge should be a supporter under the Advocates Act, 1961 with 10 years of involvement, or an official of the Indian Legal Service. It leaves the qualifications for accreditation of arbitrators is proposed to be endorsed by guidelines to be outlined by a discretion council to be set up. It further expresses that if an Award is being given based on a fake arrangement or debasement, at that point the court can give an unqualified stay up to an allure under Section 34 of the intervention law is forthcoming.

A better position for Arbitrator's in the Status Quo

The Indian Judicial position, keeping in mind, that as an arbitrator and parties are to exist in such a relation that the presence or role of each should not adversely affect the other, has brought out effective judicial precedents to make better such position, not only in terms of prevention of conflict of interest by mentioning an exhaustive list of grounds under the Fifth and Seventh Schedule of the Act, giving affected parties the right to challenge such appointment in case of pre-existing relationships between parties and arbitrators, but also putting an end, to appointment of sole arbitrators, and ensuring appointment of qualified arbitrators with sound knowledge of International Law for effective adjudication.

Historically, in India, several public sector undertakings (PSUs) have provided for an arbitration clause to refer all disputes to an arbitration to be heard by the person holding a certain position in the PSU (e.g., a general manager). In the past, such clauses were upheld to be valid by the Indian courts.

In Assignia-Vil JV v. Rail Vikas Nigam Ltd.[45], the Delhi High Court was confronted with a circumstance wherein the parties had gone into a long-term construction contract and had alluded certain questions to mediation. This discretion was before arbitrators who involved resigned and serving representatives of the respondent. During the pendency of this intervention and the exhibition of the contract, certain further debates emerged. Besides, and during this mediating period, the new amendments to the Act got powerful. Assignia-Vil JV in this way moved toward the Delhi High Court looking for the arrangement of an autonomous board of arbitrators (i.e., arbitrators that didn't involve serving representatives and ex-workers). The respondent fought that the issues concerning the new debate ought to be alluded to the primary council, which was at that point comprised and hearing the past discretion. The Delhi High Court took a realistic view, notwithstanding, holding that these were new questions and that the intervention had been conjured after the new enactment had come into power. The Court accordingly held for a new council being comprised.

However, in The Government of Haryana PWD Haryana (B and R) Branch v. M/s GF Toll Road Pvt. Ltd. and Ors.[46], the Supreme Court of India had before it a pre-requisite mediation wherein the public works division (PWD) of the Haryana government had tested the choice not to allow the PWD to name an ex-worker as its candidate mediator. The Supreme Court thought about the principal section in Fifth Schedule of the Act and held that, while there was an unmistakable bar to a current representative from acting as an authority, there is no programmed bar on account of an ex-worker, and that this would need to be tried under the norm of sensible anxiety of predisposition. The Court held that there was no such case made out, particularly since the resigned representative being referred to had resigned almost 10 years before his selection as an authority.

Further, on account of Perkins Eastman Architects DPC and Anr. v. HSCC India Ltd.[47], the Supreme Court had before it a Section 11 application wherein it needed to consider the legitimacy of the authority of the respondent's overseeing chief to name the sole judge. The Court held that an individual who has an interest in the result of a mediation should not be enabled to designate the sole mediator. The Supreme Court additionally explained in its resulting judgment on account of Proddatur Cable TV Digi Services v. Siti Cable Network Ltd.[48] that the judgment in the Perkin Eastman case would likewise apply to progressing mediations that were being directed under the Act as revised by the 2015 Amendment Act.

Conclusion

After the 2019 Amendment Act with the normal turning of the 2021 Bill to a law soon, the Indian Legal Position is supposed to be most appropriate to achieve equality among all the partners in the mediation cycle, by permitting all the partners get a chance to look for unqualified stay on authorization of arbitral awards where the arrangement or contract is "incited by misrepresentation or debasement". Further, checking abuse of the arrangements under Arbitration and Conciliation Act, 1996 would set aside the citizens cash by considering those responsible who redirected of them unlawfully.

The Indian legal position has been gaining predictable ground, be that as it may, the street till here has not been totally smooth. With the advancement, some new hazy situations have arisen in the mess encompassing International Commercial Arbitrations. For example, as talked about in detail hereinbefore, the inclusion of the stipulation to Section 2(2) of the Act, which makes Sections 9, 27 and 37(1) and (3) of the Act the special cases for decide that Part I will just apply to India-situated assertions and is dependent upon an arrangement between the parties despite what might be expected, has caused a dissimilarity of assessment. The courts have figured out how to set down justification for determining parties' verifiable/unequivocal aim to bar the pertinence of Part I all in all. However, contradictory rulings of the High Courts show that there is no such procedure to decide whether the parties expected to bar the use of the absolved sections, and it appears probable that the investigation will be appealed to the Supreme Court in the coming years.

Courts and the Union Legislature have acted with a view to getting Indian arbitration law into line with international best practice. With the pro-arbitration stance of the courts and the 2015 and 2019 Reform Acts in force, there is reason to look forward to the implementation of these best practices in the Indian Arbitration Act in the near future.

[1] Raghavan, Vikram, *New Horizons for Alternative Dispute Resolution in India: The New Arbitration Law of 1996*. 13 J. Int'l Arb. 5, 9-24 (No. 4, 1996).

[2] R.M. Investment & Trading Co. (P) Ltd. v. Boeing Co., (1999) 5 SCC 108.

[3] Bharat Aluminium Co. v. Kaiser Aluminium Technical Services Inc., (2012) 9 SCC 552.

[4] Bhatia International v. Bulk Trading SA, 2002 (4) SCC 105.

[5] Harmony Innovation Shipping Ltd. v. Gupta Coal India Ltd., 2015 (3) SCALE 295.

[6] Enercon (India) Ltd. & Ors v. Enercon GmbH & Anr, (2014) 5 SCC 1.

[7] Korp Gems (India) Pvt. Ltd. v. Precious Diamond Ltd., 2007 (3) ArbLR 32.

[8] Chloro Controls (I) P. Ltd. v. Severn Trent Water Purification Inc. & Ors., 2013 (1) SCC 641.

[9] Promod Nair, *A Sixty Month Makeover: Reinventing India as an 'Arbitration Friendly ' Jurisdiction*, Kluwer Arbitration Blog (May 10, 2011), available at: http://kluwerarbitrationblog.com/2011/05/10/ reinventing-india-as-an-arbitration-friendly-jurisdiction/.

[10] Parliament of India, Lok Sabha Debates Vol XIV, Sixth Session, 2015/1937 (Saka), No 16, 156.

[11] Union of India v. MS Singh Builders, (2009) 4 SCC 523.

[12] Naren Karunakaran, *How India Inc. Is Coping with Ineffective Ad-Hoc Arbitration and Paving Way for a New Trend*, The Economic Times (Sep. 2015), available at: http://economictimes.indiatimes.com/news/company/corporate-trends/how-india-inc-is-coping-with-ineffective-ad-hoc-arbitration-and-paving-way-for-a-new-trend/articleshow/47996642.cms.

[13] RM Investment & Trading v. Boeing, AIR 1994 SC 1136.

[14] Khardah Corporation v. Raymon & Co., AIR 1962 SC 1810.

[15] Virgoz Oils and Fats Ltd. v. National Agricultural Marketing Federation of India, 2016 SCC OnLine Del 6203

[16] Koch Navigation v. Hindustan Petroleum Corp., AIR 1989 SC 2198.

[17]*Supra Note* 4.

[18] Venture Global Engineering v. Satyam Computers Services Ltd., (2008) 4 S.C.C. 190.

[19] Bharat Aluminum Co. v. Kaiser Aluminum Technical Services Inc., (2012) 9 S.C.C. 552.

[20] ONGC Ltd. v. Saw Pipes Ltd., (2003) 5 S.C.C. 705.

[21] Anandji Haridas v. State of Gujarat, (1977) 0 G.L.R. 271.

[22] Aditya Sondhi, *Arbitration in India: Some Myths Dispelled*, 19(2) Student Bar Review (2007).

[23] Shri Lal Mahal Ltd. v. Progeto Grano Spa, 2014 (2) SCC 433.

[24]*Supra Note* 4.

[25] Law Commission of India, 176th Report on Arbitration and Conciliation (Amendment) Act (2001).

[26] The Arbitration and Conciliation Act, sec. 36 (1996).

[27] Centrotrade Minerals & Metals Inc. v. Hindustan Copper Ltd., 11 SCC 245 (2006).

[28] B. Shama Rao v. Union Territory of Pondicherry, AIR 1480 SC (1967).

[29] Commissioner of Income-tax, Bombay v. M/s Amritlal Bhogilal and Co., AIR 868 SC 868 (1958).

[30]*Id.*

[31] Bhavnagar University v. Palitana Sugar Mill (P) Ltd. and Ors., 2 SCC 111 (2003).

[32] The Arbitration and Conciliation Act, sec. 34 (1996).

[33] Fazalally Jivaji Raja v. Khimji Poonji and Co., AIR 476 Bom (1934).

[34] Centrotrade Minerals & Metals Inc. v. Hindustan Copper Ltd. 11 SCC 245 (2006).

[35] Balvant N. Viswamitra and Ors. v. Yadav Sadashiv Mule (Dead) through LRS. and Ors., 3 SCC 4377 (2004).

[36] Liverpool & London S.P. & I Asson. Ltd. v. M.V. Sea Success I 9 SCC 512 (2004).

[37] The Arbitration and Conciliation Act, sec. 35 (1996).

[38] Hiralal Agarwalla & Co. v. Jokin Nahopier & Co., AIR 647 Cal (1927).

[39] O.P. Malhotra, *The Scope of Public Policy under the Arbitration and Conciliation Act*, 1996, 19 Students

Bar Review 2 23 (2007).

[40] Alexis Mourre & Luca G. Brozolo, *Towards Finality of Arbitral Awards: Two Steps Forward and One Step*

Back, 2 Journal of International Arbitration 23 (2006).

[41] Guy Robin, *The Advantages and Disadvantages of International Commercial Arbitration*, 2014 Int'l Bus. L.J.

152 (2014).

[42] William K. II Slate, *Cost and Time Effectiveness of Arbitration*, 3 CONTEMP. ASIA ARB. J., 182, 186, 190 (2010).

[43] Union of India v. Singh Builders Syndicate 4 SCC 523(2009).

[44] Centrotrade Minerals & Metals Inc. v. Hindustan Copper Ltd. 11 SCC 245 (2006).

[45] Assignia-Vil JV v. Rail Vikas Nigam Ltd., Arbitration Petition No. 677 of 2015.

[46] The Government of Haryana PWD Haryana (B and R) Branch v. M/s. G.F. Toll Road Pvt. Ltd. & Ors., (2019) CIVIL APPEAL NO. 27/2019 (Supreme Court of India).

[47] Perkins Eastman Architects DPC v. HSCC (India) Ltd., 2019 SCC Online 1517.

[48] Proddatur Cable TV DIGI Services v. SITI Cable Network Limited, O.M.P.(T)(COMM.)109/2019.

CHAPTER TWO

REGULATION OF SPACs IN INDIA: AN ANALYSIS OF THE CONCERNS AND THE WAY FORWARD

Introduction

The Special Purpose Acquisition Companies (hereinafter "SPACs") have wreaked havoc on the American financial markets. The modus operandi remains simple: a management team or a separate business is formed to look for prospective private equity investments that it can purchase and then sell to the public. The SPAC raises money from the general public in the same way that a corporation raises money via various methods such as an Initial Public Offering (hereinafter "IPO") or a Follow-on Public Offering (hereinafter "FPO"). However, the SPAC does not need to use these methods to generate donations, and as a consequence, it saves money, time, and avoids public scrutiny. One of India's key difficulties in regard to the SPAC economy is the latter, i.e. a lack of public oversight. This is an area where the regulatory framework is, for the most part, deafeningly mute.

Regulatory concerns under The Companies Act

The Companies Act, 2013[1] has established the most rigorous regulatory concern in the issue of the SPACs proposal. SPACs may have made a resurgence on Wall Street and in international capital markets, but entering the Indian market will be difficult due to the Act's restriction. The SPACs' reserve-to-IPO strategy clearly violates a number of regulatory bodies. It is important to note that SPACs have a time restriction of 18-24 months to execute transactions, although under the Act's principles, the registrar of companies has the authority to remove a company's name if it does not initiate any business operations within one year of its registration. As a result, the registrar made a number of operational judgments invalidating numerous shell firms, including the timetable for completing the De-SPAC transition, which may be insufficient to fulfil the Act's requirements. To effectively sustain SPAC and claim some exemptions, companies should be permitted to deliver a notification to the Registrar of Companies disclosing that the sole purpose of their incorporation is to raise capital and that the SPAC has no business objective to initiate within one year of its incorporation. If SPACs are to be successful in India, the Act must be changed to avoid legal difficulties for the company's management and definite uncertainty for shell firms.

Concerns surrounding Antitrust and Mergers & Acquisitions

Concerns about competition law arise from a similar thread of having a hazy or non-existent operational history. Furthermore, in order to carry out the Competition Act, 2002[2], the Competition Commission of India (hereinafter "CCI") requires jurisdiction over companies (or entrants) such as SPAC structures depending on their jurisdiction origins. Assume that these SPAC firms (which were formed through reverse mergers or acquisitions of Indian corporations and then went public) had a strong presence in India.[3] In that situation, they may be able to raise competition issues in this market. Furthermore, even if they do not have a large presence in India, they may still have an impact on competition through reverse mergers and strategic acquisitions. As a result, it is apparent that the CCI and applicable M&A legislation must be applied to these SPAC businesses.

All of this necessitates extensive disclosures from the SPAC management or special business on a variety of topics, such as transactions, potential acquisitions, and the voting right power dynamics following the proposed purchase, among other things. India's effort and money spent on the SPAC listing has increased substantially as a result of these disclosures (if possible, from the security law end of the requirements). Due to the lack of required compliance with these requirements, SPAC companies may be hesitant to make these disclosures. Apart from that, these disclosures are frequently sensitive, and the target business does not always make a decision at the start of the SPAC creation. Instead, the modus operandi is such that, once a SPAC is established, it is promoted (or disseminated) to the general public as a way for them to park their assets in private equity. After that, a target is painstakingly picked using adequate due diligence. As a result, it may not be evident at the time of listing, and SPACs may not be in a position to provide such disclosures.

SPACs and the Indian Capital Markets

Importantly, the SPAC is not qualified for an IPO due to SEBI restrictions. Companies must have net tangible assets of at least 3 crores in the preceding three years, least average combined pre-tax functional returns of 15 crores in any three of the prior five years, and net worth of at least 1 crore in each of the last three years, according to SEBI Regulation 6(1)[4].

A business that does not fulfil the aforementioned requirements for primary listing, on the other hand, may apply for listing provided it follows the alternative listing rules set out in Regulations 6(2)[5] and 32(2)[6]. These regulations allow firms to express their segments toward a public offering by only selling if the issue occurs throughout the book building process and at least 75% of the net offer is allocated to qualified institutional purchasers.

Furthermore, the market regulator SEBI has taken into account the recent expansion of the startup business and the challenges it faces, as well as the creation of an Innovators Growth Platform. Having stated that, the platform permits a business to list provided institutional investors meet their 25% capital criteria for at least one year prior to the offering; nevertheless, the delisting instructions are generic in nature, and the platform has yet to face any company listing.

The SEBI should take into consideration the industry's changing dynamics as well as international market authorities such as the Securities and Exchange Commission of the United States, which oversee SPAC transactions. In January of this year, the US stock market countered economic growth by raising $26 billion.

Furthermore, the International Financial Services Centre's Authority released a Consultation Paper[7] on the issuance and listing of securities, which included the SPACs listing formulas. To SEBI's Primary Market Advisory Committee for the framework of SPACs listing in India, the paper serves as ideas for efficient inspection for Pro-SPAC rules. The scope of the offer, the minimum requirement, the minimum subscription, and the particular duties of the SPAC are all detailed in the agreement, which includes a three-year purchase term that is renewed for one year. Act as a forecast for the procedural aspects of the law that will be issued and reviewed by regulators.

Conclusion

Regulators should not leave firms high and dry after such a dramatic transformation, or in a downward cycle exacerbated by regulation. The main goal should be to create a structure that can remove the jurisprudential and regulatory haze, regardless of the dangers. Even if the current regulatory squabble ends, the consequences will be difficult to overcome due to the high expense of executing the tax dilemma and stamp duty requirements, which operate as anti-SPAC laws.

Furthermore, if India's legal framework for SPACs is established, it would open up a slew of new options for local businesses and startups to access the Indian capital markets, which will be critical to the country's economic progress. It's worth noting that there's a steady stream of Indian businesses reaching the unicorn club and choosing for international listings since they're not qualified to list in the Indian market. More profit, higher values, worldwide awareness, and foreign direct investment might all result from the growth.

[1] Ministry of Corporate Affairs, The Companies Act (2013).

[2] Competition Commission of India, The Competition Act (2002).

[3] The Competition Act, sec. 5 (2002).

[4] Securities and Exchange Board of India (Issue of Capital and Disclosure Requirements) Regulations, Regulation 6(1) (2018).

[5]*Id.*, Regulation 6(2).

[6]*Id.*, Regulation 32(2).

[7] International Financial Services Centres Authority, *Consultation paper on the proposed IFSCA (Issuance and Listing of Securities) Regulations* (2021).

CHAPTER THREE

QUO VADIS INDIAN ARBITRATION AND THE INDIAN CORPORATE SECTOR: A CRITICAL STUDY OF THE STATUS QUO OF ARBITRABILITY OF CORPORATE DISPUTES

Introduction

The Government of India has recently accepted the fact that litigation has flooded specialised tribunals like the National Company Law Tribunal (hereinafter "NCLT") and the National Company Law Appellate Tribunal (hereinafter "NCLAT"), devised to settle conflicts in the business sector. Recognizing the same, the legislature has taken measures. The decriminalisation of such company law conflicts and giving them a civil colour is one such initiative.

A committee created under the chairmanship of Mr. Injeti Srinivas submitted its report to the Ministry of Corporate Affairs on 14 August 2018, entitled Report of the Committee to Investigate Offences under the Companies Act, 2013. One of the Committee's key recommendations was to re-categorize 16 out of 81 offences in the compoundable offence category into an in-house adjudication framework in which defaults would be subject to a penalty levied by the adjudicating officer.

The 2019 changes were implemented in the Companies Act, 2013, following the submission of the committee's recommendations to the MCA[1], which whittled down the rigours of criminal incarceration and fines for administrative lapses and incorporated the rules for levying punishments into an in-house adjudication process,[2] moving certain cases from NCLT and NCLAT to in-house adjudication, giving these offences a civil color.

In order to explain the raison d'être of this article, in situations concerning business conflicts, one needs to understand the complications of the justice system. In the case of business conflicts, the case-loads have long ago been burdened by the NCLT and NCLAT being the sole forum. The free-flow of justice has been obstructed by minor and insignificant incidents of non-compliance and administrative anomalies. This delayed complaint processing results in an increased logistical workload and a burden on the economy. The deterrent that the sentences can bring melts out in thin air once the time involved in litigation is extended. The expert committee appointed by the Ministry of Corporate Affairs (MCA) has acknowledged and discussed this part of the clogged tribunals time and again. The predecessors of the Injeti Srinivas Report, namely the Shardul Shroff Committee (2001)[3], Irani Committee (2005)[4], and the 21st Standing Committee on Finance (2010)[5] had recommended that civil penalties be prescribed for transgressions which are purely procedural in nature and a broader outlook to be taken up in such scenarios and such technical deviations should be dealt under an in-house mechanism designed for levying penalties in case of technical defaults.

The debates and introspections surrounding the suitability of arbitration as a forum for settling intra-corporate conflicts have taken centre stage alongside the drumbeats of headlines heralding the changes to the Companies Act. Traditionally, business cases have become the state courts' exclusive venue, but with the increasing origins of arbitration, the question arises if these roots will bear fruit in disputes over corporate law.

This article sheds some light on the relevant problems that arise when the worlds of business and arbitration collide. It paves a way for arbitration to be welcomed in the corporate world, and explains why much awaits its arrival. In terms of judicial pronouncements on how to involve arbitration of corporate affairs and conflicts arising out of them, the author will scrutinise the arbitrability of intra-corporate disputes. Finally, this article will analyse the arbitrability of allegations of injustice and mismanagement and find out that not only is the new legal situation asynchronous, yet often misplaced.

Is arbitration needed for the newly decriminalised offences?

The report of the Injeti Srinivas Committee contained few clauses pertaining to failure to meet with corporate governance principles that separated them into serious and non-serious crimes and then concluded that the latter were readily observable and thus did not warrant a proper criminal trial. As a result, they recommended that certain crimes be decriminalised and punished by penalties and not fines. In addition, it was recommended that in-house adjudication be forwarded to them.

These offences include offences under Section 53(3) (Prohibition on the issuance of discount shares), Section 165(6) (Acceptance of directorships above a defined limit), Section 191(5) (Payment to directors not to be rendered in the event of loss of office, except under certain cases and according to the limitations laid down. Any sum earned by the director shall be kept in trust), Section 197 (15) (Overall full management remuneration and management remuneration in the absence or inadequacy of profits) and Section 203 (5) (Overall maximum management remuneration and management remuneration in the absence or inadequacy of profits) (Appointment of key managerial personnel in certain classes of companies).

It is foreseeable that as such, penal laws have transitioned into civil provisions parties would try to include them under the ambit of arbitration agreements. The authors are of the view there is no need or practicality of pushing arbitration herein because of the following reasons:

Absence of a Second Party

In spite of the implicit protections in the rules, except for the wrongdoer on account of the discoverability and quick identification of such defaults,[6] the above-mentioned violations were placed under the in-house adjudication after the 2019 amendment, which corrected them by enforcing penalties.[7]

According to the law provided for in Section 7 of the Arbitration and Conciliation Act, 1996, certain clauses are merely non-compliance on the part of the corporation, there is an absence of a second party, rendering them nearly impossible to arbitrate.

Efficiency and effectiveness of introducing arbitral mechanism

The revised regulations are slight technical defaults or procedural lapses which the adjudicating officer can readily cope with. In order to provide a timely settlement of such conflicts, these amendments were made.[8] Pushing arbitration for such disputes would further prolong the time required, as time-consuming steps are the appointment of the arbitrator, the selection of the seat of arbitration, etc.[9]

In comparison, arbitration needs a reasonable sum of money to be spent at all points, and looking at cost benefit analyses relative to the amount of penalties potentially owed for non-compliance, the writers argue that arbitration is not a viable solution to court litigation and welcome the reforms to include a simple and cost-effective alternative.

Modus of introducing arbitration in Intra-corporate Disputes

A shareholder arrangement combined with a corporation's AoA regulates a shareholder's relationship with a firm and continues to control conflicts between the same parties. The conflict arising from the arrangement of owners or the constitution of the corporation is clearly contractual and may be appealed to arbitration.

The minority shareholders are generally hanging on the pity of the majority anytime an intra-corporate disagreement occurs, and appear to seek refuge from the shareholder arrangement or the company's constitution that might have an arbitration provision. The Special Courts have currently declined to offer a speedy recovery from such conflicts, and thus arbitration no longer fits the shareholders' interest. In India, it is established that explicit consent from both parties should be given in order to make reference to arbitration.[10]

In arbitration, the term 'mandatory' sounds like a threat to the requirement of free consent. The requirement of explicit consent, however, is not necessarily undermined by the mandatory shareholder agreement because the shareholders have to vote for it whenever this proposal is raised, and those who do not like the idea of arbitrating the forthcoming disputes may choose to vote against it. In addition, they will not let their shares go or acknowledge that they are bound by the arbitration agreement. In addition, the clause will be in the official document, which makes it practically necessary to be known about it by prospective shareholders. Considering this knowledge, they may make their decision and accept the agreement accordingly.

The question which now arises is whether the Indian Laws allow for such mandatory shareholder arbitrations. The Companies Act, 2013 and the Securities and Exchange Board of India Act 1992 (SEBI) are the potential hurdles before the implementation of Mandatory Shareholders Arbitrations (MSA). A clear reading of Section 36(1) of the Companies Act, 2013, provides for the presumption that the Articles of Association form a legal arrangement of which the corporation and its representatives are partners. The MSA may be enforced by replicating the dispute settlement clause of a company's articles of incorporation or by a private shareholder arrangement.[11] Yet Section 9 of the 2013 Companies Act lays down that the terms of the memorandum or articles of association will be overridden by the Companies Act. Therefore, if a disagreement occurs and the clause of the terms of association goes against the sole authority of NCLT or NCLAT[12], it is not possible to impose an arbitration arrangement, except under some cases.[13]

The arbitration clause of the Articles of Association varies from the arbitration clause of the Commercial Contracts, the customary procedure and the law requiring the parties to define the issues in terms of which the arbitration clause may be based upon. However, in the articles of association, these requirements are missing because they are only instructions for the company's administration matters. In the case of Khushiram v. Honutal, the High Court of Kolkata ruled that the arbitration provision could be invoked only if a conflict occurred between the members of the company's close association. In the case of Shiv Omkar v. Bansidhar Jagannath, where the Bombay High Court claimed that the conflict is arbitrable if the transaction that initiated the dispute is beyond the confines of the article of association, this was further echoed.

The Securities and Exchange Board of India Act (hereinafter "SEBI Act") is the second challenge before the MSA, it deals with the matters of securities that have a huge influence on the public and economic development. It is an existing rule where the decision is absolutely vested in the possession of the special body referring it for arbitration as there is a law overseeing particular rights and responsibilities, it would be contrary to public policy if securities that have a significant effect on public and economic growth.[14]

In view of this, it is evident that there is a ban on securities conflict arbitration, but the SEBI itself has adopted some principles that facilitate arbitration in related disputes. SEBI's circulars are released and set out the principles and procedures for remedying investor complaints.

In addition, SEBI bylaws have arrangements to settle conflicts resulting from trade between members through arbitration. Related clauses can also be included in the National Stock Exchange by-laws.

Conclusion

The unending pressure on the Special Courts has led the lawmakers and courts to find a viable way to mitigate the duties placed on NCLT and NCLAT. In order to make the functioning of the Special Courts plain sailing, the lawmakers have consistently taken up numerous changes. The decriminalisation of minor bureaucratic lapses and technical defaults was one of those exceptional reforms.

The author concludes that in-house adjudication of such disputes is the optimal mechanism, after proper analysis of all the conflict settlement mechanism with respect to the recently revised clauses, the other two key solutions, including circuit courts and arbitration, will entail costs and are unjustified. The lawmakers are also trying to make India appropriate for commercial activities, and a new committee has recently been appointed to further strengthen the Companies Act to turn more criminal legislation into civil provisions.

The author recommended sending more and more disputes to arbitration and expanding the reach of arbitrable disputes as the only way for the courts to decrease the number of cases going to the NCLT and

NCLAT. In addition, a flexible approach to adjudicating the arbitrability of intra-corporate disputes should be introduced to enable the courts to use statutory shareholder arbitration to do so.

[1] The Companies (Amendment) Act, 2009.

[2] Companies (Adjudication of Penalties) Rules, §3 (2019).

[3] Executive Summary 2001, Ministry of Finance (Sep 5, 2020, 12:20 AM) available at: https://www.finmin.nic.in/sites/default/files/chandra.pdf.

[4] Report on Company Law 2005 (Oct. 6, 2020, 10:25 AM) http://www.primedirectors.com/pdf/JJ%20Irani%20Report-MCA.pdf.

[5] The Companies Bill (2009).

[6] Report of the Committee to Review Offences under the Companies Act, 2013, 24, available at: http://www.mca.gov.in/Ministry/pdf/ReportCommittee_28082018.pdf.

[7] Companies Act, § 165(6), § 53(3), § 191(5), § 197(15), § 203(5) (2013).

[8] *Supra Note* 7, 44.

[9] The Arbitration and Conciliation (Amendment) Act, §29A (2015).

[10] Afcons Infrastructure Ltd. v. Cherian Varkey Construction Co. (P) Ltd., (2010) 8 SCC 24.

[11] International Bar Association, *IBA Guide on Shareholders' Agreement*, (October 1, 2019), available at: http://www.shareholderagreementweb.com/form/415828012-Raja-Sujith.

[12] O.P.Gupta v. Shiv General Finance (P.) Ltd 1975 SCC OnLine Del 147.

[13] Khusiram v. Honutmal, 53 CWN 505 (H).

[14] Kingfisher Airlines Limited vs Capt. Prithvi Malhotra Instructor, 2012 SCC OnLine Bom 1704.

CHAPTER FOUR

THE TUSSLE BETWEEN E-COMMERCE STORES AND PHYSICAL STORES

Background

Retailers in physical shops employ a significant portion of the population, and a greater portion of the population is reliant on them. However, the introduction of e-stores, with their appealing incentives and vast selection, has slapped the dread of uncertainty and powerlessness in their faces.

The Indian retail industry, which is the third biggest in Asia and the fourth largest in the world, is projected to reach USD 1.2 trillion by the end of 2021 and USD 1.75 trillion by 2026, with domestic retail sales growing at a CAGR of 10.8% between 2021 and 2022. Unorganized retail, such as traditional family-run neighbourhood stores, and organised retail, such as brick-and-mortar big retailers and internet shopping sites, make up the retail market.

The development of e-commerce in India has been fueled by rising internet penetration and the usage of smartphones and social media. Exorbitant real estate prices, high operating expenses, and a scarcity of suitable retail locations have hampered the development of bigger physical shops, pushing major retailers to resort to e-commerce platforms as a growth channel in addition to their websites and existing physical stores, if any. Due to services like cash-on-delivery and free home delivery, significant discounts, flexible payment choices and buy-back policies, and the availability of a broad range of goods, e-commerce has grown more popular, especially in Tier II and Tier III cities.

The study of known determinants of online purchasing behaviour is especially important during the COVID-19 pandemic, since businesses must predict consumer behaviour to retain a competitive advantage throughout this worldwide catastrophe.

This part attempts to study the different ways in which retail companies are being impacted, as well as the various recovery strategies that they are devising to combat those e-stores in their fight for existence. This study also examines the impact of the growing popularity of online shopping on the profitability of different businesses. Despite the study's lack of regularity, an effective effort has been made to illuminate the situation and provide specific recommendations.

Introduction

Online buying has grown at a breakneck pace over the past decade, owing to the fact that it is a more cost-effective and convenient alternative to conventional shopping.

Nonetheless, the shift from one to another, more contemporary purchasing method initially caused consumers to be concerned about the following: personal information leakage, online fraud, discrepancy between the purchased product quality and the desired quality, failed delivery, and so on. These worries are now far less prevalent, as consumers have seen the benefits of internet purchasing.[1] Consumers can buy anything at any time without actually going to the store; consumers can find the same product at a lower price by comparing multiple websites at the same time; consumers want to avoid feeling pressured when communicating face-to-face with the retailer; consumers want to avoid traffic jams that can o Consumers benefit from additional information and chances to compare goods and prices while shopping online, as well as increased product variety, convenience, and simplicity of locating desired products. Online shopping, it has been claimed, provides greater pleasure to contemporary customers seeking ease and quickness. When a customer sees a banner ad or an online promotion in online communication, it may draw their attention and pique their interest in the advertised goods. The consumer may request more information before making a purchasing decision. If there is insufficient information, they will seek for it online, for example, via online catalogues, websites, or search engines.

Retaining online customers has gotten a lot of attention since it's a way to acquire a competitive edge. Customers who are pleased with a specific online retail store will return to make further purchases. As a result, the ideas of client retention and satisfaction are becoming more essential for both online and offline businesses. As a result, it's critical to comprehend the variables that influence consumer happiness and online shop selection. The stages in the purchasing process are: problem/need identification, information search, alternative assessment, purchase decision, and post-purchase behaviour. Customer satisfaction is determined by the consumer's experience at various phases of the purchasing process.[2] Because online consumers' experiences are solely based on information provided by online stores due to the lack of physical contact with the product, it is clear that the information provided can affect consumer satisfaction, both during the information search stage and during the purchase decision stage.[3]

E-commerce, according to the United Nations Conference on Trade and Development (UNCTAD), refers to all purchases and transactions conducted via the internet or using a computer, with payment and delivery options available both online and offline. Business to business (B2B), business to customer (B2C), customer to customer (C2C), and business to government (B2G) interactions are all examples of e-commerce.

Official data on the value of domestic and cross-border e-commerce are currently unavailable. Only a few nations have gathered data on e-commerce earnings. The majority of the data available on the growth of global e-commerce originates from private consultancy surveys or estimates from relevant authorities.

Governments across the globe are putting a lot of effort into promoting computer literacy so that every person may take part in the global digital society. Digital literacy is defined by the United Nations Educational, Scientific, and Cultural Organization as the ability to safely and appropriately access, manage, understand, integrate, communicate, evaluate, and create information through digital technologies for employment, decent jobs, and entrepreneurship. Computer literacy, ICT literacy, information literacy, and media literacy are all terms used to describe a set of skills. Citizens' participation in the digital society leads to an increase in social and material well-being, which is aided by the availability of e-commerce.

Adopting digital technology and e-commerce methods may help small-format businesses expand their client base. Furthermore, digitisation improves their creditworthiness by generating data via the use of point-of-sale (POS) devices, digital payments, and debit and credit payments, which helps lenders issue loans. For kirana shops, digitisation will include a switch from cash to digital/online payments, the use of applications to manage operations (inventory, invoicing, and financing), and integration with the e-commerce industry.

Growth of E-Commerce Platforms

The digital economy and e-commerce are becoming more important in attempts to fulfil the Sustainable Development Goals, bringing with them new possibilities as well as new difficulties. As UNCTAD's Information/ Digital Economy Reports and other international studies have demonstrated, the facilitation and exploitation of these digital advances will be critical to future economic success in all nations. The shift to a digital economy, in which information and communications technologies (ICTs) play an increasingly important role in the production, consumption, and exchange of the majority of products and services, has accelerated in the past decade. Because of variations in definition and measurement difficulties, estimates of the size of the digital economy range from 4.5 to 15.5 percent of global GDP, while the proportion of digitally provided services in total service exports has grown from 45 percent to 52 percent between 2005 and 2019.[4] This shift has been unevenly distributed, but it has been faster and more broad in industrialised and high-income emerging nations than in other regions. E-commerce has the ability to broaden the breadth and geographic reach of trade possibilities for developing nations, as well as increase the variety of existing and new companies. In domestic markets, it also plays an increasingly significant role in the supply and distribution of both products and services. However, a variety of obstacles in infrastructure, financing, resources, and governance are impeding the development of e-commerce in many developing nations. Countries that overcome these obstacles and create enabling frameworks for e-commerce will be better positioned to capitalise on its potential benefits and address challenges both domestically and internationally, whereas those that do not risk becoming less dynamic at home and less competitive abroad. In the absence of policies to capitalise on e-commerce, there is a danger that digital advances may exacerbate inequality rather than promote fairness.

During the year 2020, the COVID-19 epidemic has dominated worldwide economic growth. Movement restrictions and other public health measures have slowed economic activity in most sectors and nations, impacting production, distribution, and consumption. The global economy is expected to contract by at least 4% this year, rather than expand by 4% or more as originally forecast. In May 2020, global commerce in goods dropped by almost 18%. (compared with the same month in 2019). Recessions in global economic activity put developing and lower-developed nations, as well as their people, at risk.[5]

E-commerce and other information and communication technologies have diminished the significance of time as a determinant of economic and social activity structure. It has the potential to save time by allowing customers to buy more effectively, but it also has the potential to decrease leisure time due to the technology's ability to offer a constant electronic connection to work. Because many e-commerce goods (for example, entertainment) are interactive and need rapid consumption, a deeper understanding of the effect of e-commerce and ICTs on time usage is required.

While technical progress is occurring at an amazing and increasing rate, achieving understanding and agreement, particularly on social problems, takes time. Because of the speed and fluidity of the Internet, it is necessary to rethink the most effective method to rule and if centralised decision-making can keep up. This indicates that decentralised decision-making systems, such as self-regulatory mechanisms, should be considered. Another approach is to explore speed control techniques such as "putting sand into the wheels." This emphasises the need of gaining a better knowledge of how quicker and more interconnected exchanges affect people, organisations, governments, and communities.

Competition regulation will have to confront new kinds of anti-competitive behaviour as the ease of establishing business networks grows, conventional market borders blur, and technology weakens the justification for the monopolistic advantages given to many service activities. Non-rivalry (one person's consumption does not restrict or diminish the value of a product to other customers), network externalities (each new user of a product enhances its worth to other users), and rising returns to scale are all advantages for many e-commerce goods (unit costs decrease as sales increase). These characteristics create an atmosphere in which producers may attempt to participate in activities that allow them to become the de facto standard, or at least a portion of it. This has the potential to stifle innovation and competitiveness.[6]

The WTO is looking at ways to include goods purchased and sold via internet commerce into current trade laws. E-commerce will boost international trade, especially in electronically delivered products, many of which are services that have not yet been exposed to significant international trade but have been "traded" through foreign direct investment or have only operated on a global level for large corporate clients. This shift may come as a surprise to industries that have hitherto been protected by logistical or regulatory obstacles. It will also put pressure on regulators to minimise disparities in regulatory requirements, certification, licencing, and activity limitations for newly traded goods.[7]

For a number of factors, including its recent existence, rapid expansion from a small base, entrance and departure by a diverse range of companies (many of which are tiny and not publicly listed), and the diversity of business models being explored, Traditional economic data sources, such as government statistics agencies, have yet to collect data on internet trade. As a result, the only easily accessible data comes from e-commerce companies or market research or management consulting organisations that perform electronic commerce surveys. This may cause issues. Prior to an initial public stock offering, certain companies may try to "sell themselves." Many of them are e-commerce infrastructure providers that wish to get the activity going. Market research or management consulting companies, on the other hand, offer information and statistics regarding the present status of electronic commerce and its future prospects. They are likely to have an incentive to imply that the e-commerce industry is big and expanding quickly since they will probably expand along with it. Neither of these data sources is immune to the statistical issues that beset government statistics organisations. They seldom offer studies explaining the statistical robustness of the data, or provide details on their collecting techniques or definition of e-commerce. Because of variations in cover age, definition, and technique, some estimates differ by more than a factor of 100. While this scenario is difficult for companies considering internet commerce, they are typically experienced data consumers. They also have their own internal data gathering activities, which may serve as a check on these estimations, which most public policymakers and analysts do not have. Furthermore, the majority of projections are based on income or sales. There are three issues here. First, these figures include operating costs; this leads to double-counting because the output of one e-commerce industry (for example, Internet advertising or e-payment services) is included in the "sales" figures of other e-commerce businesses, particularly in business-to-business electronic commerce. Second, they provide little evidence that internet commerce is merely displacing sales from more conventional channels. Third, they do not disclose if companies that engage in internet trade are profitable. In reality, the vast majority of business-to-consumer electronic commerce companies aren't. This significantly restricts an examination of electronic commerce's economic effect in terms of contribution to gross domestic product (GDP) (value added). However, sales or revenues are sometimes the only measure of activity available, and although rudimentary, they do provide an indication of market size.[8]

Dominance of E-Commerce Platforms

With the capacity to supplement the initial durable good with supplementary products/services, the durable goods producer is now in a much better position to engage and interact with the consumer throughout the real use and experience stage, bolstering its position as a key decision interface. Automation, individualization, and ambient embeddedness are the main sources of value generation exploited by product platforms. The platform enables for connected consumables savings throughout the usage period by monitoring and regulating product functioning. Individual advice for optimised handling or complete automation, such as with intelligent heat and energy management, can be used to put the gathered data to good use. In terms of the purchase decision, branded product platforms may make reordering easier or more automated. They can also anticipate demand based on individual consumption habits and detect demand instantly by monitoring and managing supply. As a result, product platforms may drastically reduce the buying experience and turn it into a simple click of a button or voice confirmation of pre-made shopping lists. Purchases, particularly repurchases, may then resemble using Amazon's Dash button rather than a traditional trip to the retailer or online store. As a result, branded product platforms are becoming increasingly important as an interface for customers who make frequent, repeat purchases of products and value quick fulfilment and low friction (i.e., low-involvement decisions). Furthermore, businesses may now connect with consumers via their own interactive apps, which provide customers with portable, handy, and engaging engagement possibilities, enabling them to interact with the brand on a regular basis.[9]

Cross-selling, up-selling, and brand switching may all be possible via branded product platforms. The effectiveness of such platforms is dependent on the buying environment and product attributes: customers in low-involvement circumstances are more likely to make simple, heuristic, and spontaneous decisions based on external signals. Recommendations, targeted price discounts, and bundling may all be used by branded product platforms to encourage such choices. Low-involvement circumstances also offer less excitement, which increases the probability of consumers wanting diversity. Branded product platforms can support variety seeking by recommending new products or product categories based on preference learning.[10] Finally, for goods dominated by search attributes, consumers will benefit more from product platform-based decision making: algorithms can significantly shorten the lengthy evaluation process by quickly comparing objective features and accurately predicting the product's fit with individual preferences.

The attractiveness of a product platform is determined by how well the eco-system that emerges around it meets consumer perceived advantages via sources of value generation. As a result, integrating a variety of platform capabilities to serve a broader range of category requirements improves consumer value and increases eco-system reliance (lock-in). Game consoles, for example, have expanded their capabilities to include optical disc players, data storage devices, software stores, and video streaming platforms. Rather than being single-purpose products, they aim to become entertainment hubs. The higher the possibility of becoming a dominating consumer interface, the more value is provided by integrating the fulfilment of various category requirements.

Branded product platforms may collaborate with and join other branded product platforms to offer such complete value and encourage lock-in. A smart home system, for example, incorporates a variety of durables (e.g., refrigerators, thermostats, lights) and complements (e.g., electricity, food), and offers many advantages by monitoring consumable supply and usage, anticipating shortfalls, and automating re-purchase. Through ambient embeddedness, combining various platforms on a single physical or virtual interface, which we call a meta-platform, unlocks extra value for the consumer. Less comprehensive apps are especially vulnerable to being incorporated into a meta-platform or "system of systems," which bundles the value of linked goods into a broader need category. Integrating software directly into the physical platform is one approach to create a meta-platform. As additional durables incorporate the same software, the program's eco-system expands, allowing it to combine the usage of various goods while analysing consumer preferences across several product categories. As software advances to the heart of the eco-system, the influence of a single hardware owner is expected to dwindle. As a result, branded long-lasting platforms with little wealth generation potential from fresh sources are more likely to be owned by or merged into bigger meta-platforms. The more their owner's control over the consumer interface, the more value these meta-platforms package.[11]

Online retail platforms have effectively established themselves as a new constituency in the retailing value chain, claiming the main consumer interface. Amazon

Marketplace, Alibaba, eBay, and JD are just a few examples. These platforms use digital technology to act as middlemen between buyers and sellers in the exchange of goods and services. As a result, they are comparable to the branded product platforms discussed in the preceding paragraph in terms of economic exchange processes. These platforms, unlike branded product platforms, operate across product brands and are focused on the exchange of products rather than providing continuing post-purchase engagement value. The seller maintains sovereignty over its product offers (e.g., selection, price), while the platform owner serves as a matchmaker between the parties, which is a significant difference from institutional (online) retailing.

Many retailing sectors have been transformed by platform companies, forcing conventional players to leave the industry or contemplate far-reaching strategic changes. Competing head-to-head on product sales with fully developed retail platforms is nearly always a losing cause, necessitating transformative business model changes. As a result, platforms have taken over online retail sales. Amazon Marketplace, Amazon's platform business, accounted for more than half of all of Amazon's e-commerce sales in 2017, representing a 39 percent annual growth rate. Online retail platforms are expanding considerably quicker than institutional online or multichannel retailers due to their simple scalability at practically zero marginal costs (that is, adding another provider to the platform).[12]

Retail platforms, like other types of two-sided marketplaces, provide network effects because the platform's total value to sellers and consumers rises as the user base on both sides grows. As a consequence, big platforms tend to expand even more, while tiny rivals are driven out of the market, leading to winner-take-all results.

The sheer scale of the surviving players lays the groundwork for exploiting new forms of value generation, especially individualization and openness of product data. First, retail platforms may customise a broad range of products to specific customer requirements by combining practically infinite shelf space with sophisticated search engines. Platforms, with their greater selection depth and breadth, create better supply-demand matches than vertically integrated manufacturers or institutional retailers can.[13] This matching feature improves the relevancy of the presented product subset while also promoting savings and convenience by lowering product and transaction expenses. As a result, individualization is essential for assortment management. Second, platforms increase transparency by combining and comparing product information from many sources (e.g., pricing, features, and customer reviews), allowing consumers to make more informed decisions. Third, the retail platform can provide precise cross- and up-selling suggestions based on extensive data on consumer and seller browsing and transaction behaviour.

Retail platforms, like branded product platforms, are well-suited to combining objective, searchable data to help consumers make better decisions. Retail platforms are unusual in that they bring together an otherwise bewildering array of suppliers and product options. Consumer and professional evaluations are combined to provide some experiential information, but they lack first-hand sensory sensations and personal encounters (e.g., with service personnel or experts). As a result, the retail platform–consumer interface is less likely to dominate complicated, high-involvement, and therefore high-risk product choices. Furthermore, since retail platforms are in the "single-product" industry and cater to a wide range of categories, they are limited in their ability to provide supplementary services and complete solutions, as well as provide category-specific experiences (as branded product platforms or specialised retailers may). Rather, they play the role of a digital department store with limited capabilities for providing rich, passionate purchasing experiences. By customising the interface to their business model: quick, simple, frictionless, and product-focused, retail platforms improve efficiency. As a result, the platform–customer interaction is more effective in choice scenarios that benefit from a high level of convenience, such as regular purchases and multi-category one-stop shopping. One-stop shopping, in particular, offers online retail platforms an edge over branded product platforms, which are still limited in meeting customer requirements across categories.[14]

In a digital age, the value of physical commerce rests primarily in enabling improved decision-making and providing greater, multi-sensory experiences. That is, actual product contact and comparison still offer better informative and sensory value in a variety of purchasing scenarios, which virtual shopping can only address to a limited degree. Moreover, depending on the kind of enquiry, quick service and personal interactions may promote convenience and potential time, money, and effort savings.[15]

Consumers tend to engage in lengthy information search and depend on cognitive decision making in more involved buying circumstances, thus institutional merchants with a physical presence are particularly strong. Also, offline and multichannel methods favour goods with greater complexity and related purchasing risks, as well as those with a high prevalence of experience characteristics. Despite physical shops' continuing value-added features, internet shopping has absorbed much of the value that was previously only supplied by stationary commerce. Department shops, in particular, have seen a continuous decrease due to their broad yet limited assortments across categories. The one-stop shopping strategy, which is an important element of those shops' value offering, is far better suited to online retail platforms, which have unlimited shelves and plenty of cross-buying possibilities. Furthermore, the digital customer expects almost immediate satisfaction and is less likely to organise multi-product buying excursions. Rather, decisions are made in response to particular and very recent requirements. The value of brick-and-mortar department shops is expected to continue to decline as internet buying becomes more prevalent.[16] Physical commerce will primarily sell items defined by comprehensive and experience information search as low-involvement transactions and demand for search goods migrate online. This shift will also result in less impulsive purchasing in shops and less chances for cross-selling, both of which are essential for physical store success. Having said that, it's important to remember that there is customer heterogeneity in terms of preference for visiting brick-and-mortar stores. This implies that, despite these broad trends, a significant portion of consumers still prefers to buy in a physical store, regardless of transaction method.

Unlike department shops, specialist merchants, whether brick-and-mortar or online-only, may customise the consumer experience to a particular need category. This advantage is growing, especially for high-involvement goods, as new sources of value generation become more important. Specialization may therefore offer a competitive edge not just against traditional department stores, but also against the strength of online shopping platforms. As a result, specialised retailing is expected to grow at the cost of more general retailing formats for purchases driven by rich interactions and the requirement for high pre-purchase information transparency.[17]

The physical point of sale has also seen significant changes. When customers can purchase almost instantly from anyplace, the shop becomes essentially useless as a transaction facilitator. The key issue should therefore be how to successfully integrate and anchor the POS into the customers' purchasing experiences, rather than how to force digitalization on the POS. To put it another way, what distinguishes the physical store? The customer interface will be dominated by those who can effectively coordinate complementary value generation via physical retailing inside multichannel models. To drive loyalty and complement other transaction channels, the new physical retail environment emphasises show-rooming and customer support. Stores may reduce shop space and save money by showing just a few product variants and decreasing the number of check-out stations. As "the retail sector moves toward a concierge model focused on assisting customers, rather than focusing solely on transactions and deliveries," sales employees are freed up to enhance customer service. Designer rental business Rent the Runway and electric mobility supplier Tesla are two examples of companies that have built on the successful experience-driven retail model pioneered by Apple shops. As a result, we've seen a change in stationary retailing from transactional to experience-oriented POS. At the same time, the capacity of an experience-focused presence to generate money must be carefully preserved. Only a high-performance multichannel solution is likely to function in this scenario.

Potential Impacts

Retail's dominant control of the customer interface is being broken up by digitization, which is allowing new gatekeepers to arise. Traditional retail tasks are delegated to various players, making the development of competitive advantage based on these activities more challenging. However, digitalization creates new avenues of value creation that more efficiently meet long-standing consumer demands than previously feasible. To maintain their position in the retailing sector, the players may coordinate value generation via new sources.

Many merchants realise that they will not be able to compete effectively on pricing or selection with pure online shops or platforms in this new market. As a result, they're putting more emphasis on the consumer experience, as well as sensory and haptic engagement. This is shown by the trend toward smaller shops, pop-up stores, and experiential stores in high-frequency settings.[18] Audi, for example, is currently constructing digital showrooms in core urban areas (such as downtown London) to connect with and digitally engage consumers with the brand and product.[19] The question is whether and how merchants (and brands) can still turn those experiences into the necessary profits. In addition, the shift in physical retailing toward showrooms and service hubs necessitates the hiring of more product and technical experts, which necessitates the investment in more sophisticated personnel and training, as well as the creation of new retail jobs such as styling advisers (in fashion) and garden planners (in DIY). Furthermore, effective omnichannel touchpoint management necessitates the presence of knowledgeable specialists not only on-site, but also in the chat and contact centre.[20]

The issue of whether sensory and haptic experiences provide customers with enough value to allow merchants to compete successfully is linked to that problem. Researchers may look at how physical shops can use their unique value-creation potential to provide experiences and empower customers, allowing them to thrive in an increasingly digital environment. For example, research may be conducted to determine which of the different in-store experience characteristics (sensory, emotional, cognitive, behavioural, and relational) contribute the most to consumer value perceptions.

Many physical shops struggle to stay afloat, as shown by the many mall closures in the United States and the demise of well-known brands (Blockbuster, Radio Shack, American Apparel, ToysRUs). At the same time, shops are an important element of keeping inner cities beautiful and vibrant. Shoppers, visitors, and tourists are attracted to retailers, which subsequently patronise restaurants, attractions, and recreational facilities. Collateral consequences are quite probable when the vibrancy and attractiveness of neighbourhoods and inner cities decrease, which typically take the shape of reduced property values, higher crime rates, and less community maintenance - all of which are social expenses.

The worldwide victory march of the hard discounting idea is another element of retail structure. The success of businesses like Aldi, Lidl, and Primark can be seen in almost every mature retailing environment in the UK, US, Australia, and Europe. These formats fight fiercely on price, and they are always the lowest-priced in their respective categories. As a result, cost management is critical for these formats.[21] Most notably, these banners seldom include e-commerce operations, since they would be prohibitively costly to develop and maintain alongside physical shops. In other words, even if you don't engage in digital services, there seem to be paths to success in physical retail.

Differentiation from competitor platforms, the development of a stable, private eco-system, and the creation of a lock-in for current consumers via the platform's inherent and extrinsic advantages are all goals for branded platform owners. Value may be created via (re-)purchase opportunities, intrinsic usage values, complements, or partners. The progression of need identification and fulfilment toward genuine solution selling is particularly intriguing. Customer behaviours, interests, and experiences may be used to generate customised suggestions for whole activities, not just single items or product bundles. A travel app, for example, might evaluate user characteristics to forecast the next camping trip. It might then offer alternatives, such as how to prepare for a three-month journey to South America, as well as promote necessary gear like tents and sleeping bags. Backpacking equipment and lodging arrangements, as well as local tour suggestions and a crash course in Spanish, may be included in the offer. Another example is Adidas' Runtastic app, which, although presently restricted to monitoring and evaluating specific sports activity, has the potential to generate highly personalised training plans and equipment suggestions for marathon runners in the future. Users get increasingly locked-in to the particular eco-system as platform owners get closer to these fundamental consumer requirements. In essence, the brand guides consumers away from simple product transactions and toward more complex and continuous interactions, ultimately offering a genuine solution to their issues.

For competing brand platforms, the collateral impact of lock-in and the significance of brand equity become evident. As platforms become the main interface for engagement and getting direct access to those consumers becomes more difficult, the danger of being shut out of the customer's consideration set grows. In conventional retailing, all brands enjoyed equal access to all consumers at the moment of sale, ceteris paribus. Similarly, in the old communication environment, all brands could convey their messages via mass distribution in a fairly equitable manner. The focal consumers in the new brand platform eco-system are notoriously difficult to reach for rivals. Customers may be unaware of rival brand platforms, or purchases may be automated (e.g., Samsung's IoT-based laundry detergent re-order system). As a result, rivals often lack access to those clients for transactions or communication, and must work considerably harder to acquire genuine access to their thoughts and emotions.

Consumers are increasingly likely to participate in subscription-based and automated transactions on brand platforms. While value is created across the whole search, transaction, and consumption cycle, customers are likely to narrow their options and pay greater transaction costs than in the traditional retailing paradigm. To put it another way, a new equilibrium is likely to emerge, involving a shift from a plethora of diverse product transactions in the traditional sense to a transaction that focuses on fewer but more comprehensive brand–customer relationships, where the transaction is fully integrated into the relationship.

Online retail platforms, clearly, seem to be the major winners in the retailing landscape. Even these, however, have difficulties, which offer up new study opportunities. As exemplified by Amazon and Alibaba, these platforms frequently operate as department stores. When merchants and companies fight this tendency with more concentrated consumer connections, the platforms may suffer. Retailers and brands may provide goods with solutions, knowledge, and customised consumer experiences, and therefore act as gatekeepers for many choices made on online shopping platforms. The appeal of general platforms may also be harmed.

Online retail platforms, clearly, seem to be the major winners in the retailing landscape. Even these, however, have difficulties, which offer up new study opportunities. As exemplified by Amazon and Alibaba, these platforms frequently operate as department stores. When merchants and companies fight this tendency with more concentrated consumer connections, the platforms may suffer. Retailers and brands may provide goods with solutions, knowledge, and customised consumer experiences, and therefore act as gatekeepers for many choices made on online shopping platforms. The appeal of general platforms may also be harmed.

The ambivalence of suppliers and brands regarding their connections is another issue for platforms. Brands feel disconnected from their consumers, transaction commissions are common, and some platforms opt to offer their own versions of particular goods once they discover the income possibilities. As a result, some companies will avoid selling on such platforms, while others may exit after a bad experience with the platform. Brands, particularly big brands with sufficient power on their own, often seek methods to remain independent of such platforms.

The BRICS Scenario: A cross-jurisdictional study

Cross border E-Commerce and facilitation of trade

On a worldwide scale, cross-border e-commerce has been growing over the last 20 years. However, owing to the diverse interests and views of the BRICS, no uniform international standards for e-commerce have been created. Furthermore, no universal definition of cross-border e-commerce has been agreed upon. Only a few WTO papers, local regional trade agreements, and multilateral international accords include common cross-border e-commerce regulations. Cross-border e-commerce growth is restricted in the lack of uniform regulations, and nations participating in e-commerce are unable to profit.

In the 1990s, there was a debate over international regulations for cross-border e-commerce. In 1996, the inaugural WTO Ministerial Conference included e-commerce into the Ministerial Declaration on Trade in Information Technology Goods, whose primary goal is to lower tariffs on information technology products. In 1998, the World Trade Organization's Second Ministerial Conference approved the Global E-commerce Declaration, which defined e-commerce as a transaction using electronic methods of production, distribution, marketing, sales, and service. The WTO General Council conducted five seminars on e-commerce from 2001 to 2003, concentrating on e-commerce categorization, import tax collection, competition, jurisdiction, and legal application. The WTO Trade and Services Commission debated e-commerce transparency, domestic rules and recognition, competition and privacy protection, market access, national treatment, and tariffs, among other topics. The WTO Goods Trade Committee debated product access to e-commerce, customs valuation terms' application, import licencing processes, customs duties and other taxes, standards, and original suppliers. The World Trade Organization's Intellectual Property Committee addressed copyright protection, trademark protection, and emerging e-commerce technologies. The effect of e-commerce on developing nations and small and medium-sized businesses was addressed before the WTO Trade and Development Committee. All of the aforementioned problems are still being debated, and no uniform worldwide regulations have been established.[22]

In a global context, several BRICS nations realise the tremendous potential of e-commerce and the urgent need to unify international e-commerce regulations as soon as feasible. E-commerce has been a major problem in many international institutions, as well as a hot topic in WTO and free trade area talks. Out of the 269 regional trade clauses submitted to the WTO in March 2016, 65 are related to e-commerce. Many nations, including Brazil, have made recommendations to the World Trade Organization (WTO) regarding e-commerce regulations. Bilateral trade agreements negotiated in China in the last two years have incorporated cross-border e-commerce clauses.[23] As a result, cross-border e-commerce international laws are still in the early stages of development. In order to boost cross-border e-commerce in the future years, a greater effort for the development of uniform standards is needed.

China's net purchase via cross-border e-commerce has grown to become the world's third biggest behind the United States and the European Union in recent years. Cross-border e-commerce has also emerged as a new fuel for China's economic growth. To encourage cross-border e-commerce, China's government established the Cross-

Border E-commerce Comprehensive Pilot Zone and Cross-Border E-commerce Services Pilot Cities; in this respect, China may share its expertise with other BRICS nations. There are three major challenges to creating uniform cross-border e-commerce regulations and standards. The first is that cross-border e-commerce has an ambiguous meaning. Although cross-border e-commerce has been growing for more than two decades, the agencies have only recently made a serious attempt to establish a uniform definition. This project is still in its infancy. The United Nations International Trade Working Group defined e-commerce as "electronic commerce that completes business operations via the exchange of business information among suppliers, consumers, governments, and other players." E-commerce, according to the US government's Global E-commerce Outline, comprises transactions for commercial operations such as advertising, payment, and trade services via the Internet. Cross-border e-commerce in the United States mostly refers to digital trading. E-commerce in China include both digital and physical commodities, as well as taxes, payment, logistics, trade facilitation, and single-window digital ports. Countries have yet to agree on a single definition of cross-border e-commerce, making international regulations difficult to agree on.

The second issue with cross-border commerce is that various nations' interests are not aligned. Countries have distinct perspectives and needs when it comes to international regulations. For example, in July 2016, the United States submitted a proposal to the World Trade Organization (WTO) outlining 16 demands, including the elimination of tariffs on digital products, non-discrimination principles, cross-border data flow, free Internet, prohibiting facility localization, prohibition of forced technology transfer, protection of important source code, improved certification methods, and product tagging.[24] BRICS, like the United States, have its own set of international e-commerce laws and regulations. As a result of the disparity in interests and perspectives, conflicts are unavoidable. Finally, the BRICS' domestic legal systems are far from flawless. Traditional business is not the same as e-commerce. It inherently defies conventional time, location, and pricing constraints. Cross-border e-commerce in China has resulted in a fundamental shift in conventional international trade laws, necessitating a flawless legal framework to safeguard consumers and other sellers' rights. Even in China, existing economic and trade regulations lack the necessary conditions for e-commerce. The present legal framework is ill-equipped to deal with disputes, poor internet goods, unfair competition, and a variety of other problems. Cross-border e-commerce transactions, for example, are often modest in terms of customs transactions. China, on the other hand, lacks a regulatory framework for minor transactions. Furthermore, online transactions lack appropriate language for contracts, shopping vouchers, and service papers, resulting in a high number of conflicts. Provisions for protection are ambiguous and cannot cover the laws in industrialised nations. Furthermore, numerous new issues in the areas of cross-border e-commerce are emerging nowadays, including customs clearance, commodities inspection, tax refunds, foreign currency settlement, consumer rights, trade disputes, intellectual property, and personal information protection. These issues must be addressed by enacting novel laws and regulations. Credit, tax, regulatory, and payment systems, as well as other cross-border e-commerce systems, must be created and enhanced.[25]

Cross-border e-commerce is a new business model and a key sector for developing businesses to focus on. China's e-commerce is not only well ahead of the other BRICS nations at the moment, but it is also a key strategic sector for the future. The main policy recommendation is to rely on the WTO negotiation platform to accurately grasp the position of the five major economies, namely Europe, the United States, China, Russia, and Brazil, for future development, breaking the traditional model through key reforms, and attempting to form reciprocal international rules in the field of cross-border e-commerce as best as possible.

The goal of cross-border e-commerce development should be to achieve full electronic customs, international logistics, barrier-free information exchange, credit system transparency, and the elimination of all types of investment tariffs and policy barriers to expanding the scope of local currency settlement.[26]

To improve trade capacity, it is first essential to remove cross-border e-commerce policy obstacles. Each country's foreign exchange control, commodity definition, and commodity inspection policies are unique. Economic difficulties, political issues, and other changeable variables exist across nations. As a new online shopping model, cross-border e-commerce may occasionally avoid the collection of tariffs and intermediary taxes, leading conventional international trade to suffer. As a result, some nations raise tax barriers and erect delivery obstacles to preserve taxes and conventional commerce. In 2014, Brazil, for example, placed a 60 percent tax on incoming mail valued at more than $50 USD. Every shipment is inspected by Brazilian customs, who need business invoices, the recipient's tax ID, the declaration of goods, and other documents. Even the supply of information may be deemed fraud at times. Furthermore, several destination nations lack the necessary IT infrastructure and depend on human clearance. The efficiency is poor, which causes the distribution time to be extended. Some nations' postal systems no longer offer international scanning services for tiny parcels, making them impossible to trace. Customs signs the goods on behalf of the consumers in certain countries, and the things are no longer sent to the customers' addresses. Low tariffs must be agreed upon by all BRICS nations, as well as a simple customs processing system, payment system, and logistics system.[27]

Second, data obstacles must be eliminated. Data interoperability is a challenge for the BRICS nations. Small transactions, frequent transactions, and timeliness are all hallmarks of cross-border e-commerce. China established customs control procedures and addressed domestic clearance problems. However, China has yet to establish customs clearance and reporting interoperability with the other BRICS nations. Some nations' policies on cross-border e-commerce change often, leading businesses to suffer. It is proposed that the BRICS government agencies work together to create the World Customs Organization (WCO). It helps with customs clearance and data exchange, lowering the cost of cross-border e-commerce businesses and making the customs clearing and exit clearance processes easier.

Third, the creation of a single policy support mechanism may assist SMEs in the construction of overseas bonded warehouses. The architecture of a foreign insurance warehouse is the most straightforward method to overcome technological obstacles of cross-border e-commerce in the near run. Enterprises may utilise the foreign warehouse's inspection site as a direct delivery point or even build up a local team and subsidiaries to invest and finance in local businesses. However, specific policy support mechanisms and programmes are required. As a result, the BRICS nations may create cross-border e-commerce associations and unified cross-border e-commerce organisations to develop a common set of norms and standards. During the growth phase, cross-border e-commerce businesses may form a variety of international organisations to address common issues. It is the most effective method to bring government agencies and commercial entities together.[28]

Fourth, to incorporate e-commerce into traditional international trade, to achieve intelligent multi-language automatic switching, to achieve easy communication among buyers and sellers in different countries, and to achieve timely clearing, ordering, and payment, it is necessary to promote cross-border e-commerce and eliminate information barriers. The cost of communication may be reduced by removing information obstacles. It may also improve information flow and guarantee that various currencies are settled on time and automatically. Due to the low foreign trade threshold, SMEs may join the world market.

Fifth, the BRICS nations should work together to overcome developed countries' technological obstacles. Technology, rules, regulations, and standards, as well as the availability of sufficient information, are all areas where developing nations and industrialised countries differ in the e-commerce sector. At the same time, the governments of the BRICS should unify and create an efficient monitoring system to ensure that developed nations embrace the newest technologies. Governments should provide e-commerce businesses with appropriate information on technological trade obstacles.[29]

A concrete way forward: An individualistic and a groupistic perspective

The fundamental and objective needs of the fast growth of the BRICS national economy are BRICS national e-commerce cooperation. Not only should BRICS nations cooperate inside and amongst themselves, but they should also encourage and assist BRICS countries in reaching out to the rest of the globe. The heart and basis of BRICS e-commerce cooperation is the creation of a shared interest framework. In recent years, the BRICS nations have established a multi-faceted and multi-level cooperation mechanism, which is characterised by high-level meetings of relevant departments and reinforced by them. The member states must establish an e-business cooperation mechanism as soon as possible and strengthen capacity-building cooperation, which includes infrastructure, technology, skills, and professional training, to strengthen the BRICS economic partnership cooperation mechanism and fully prepare BRICS for e-commerce. It is also necessary to make the formation of an e-commerce alliance easier, to speed up the creation of an e-commerce access mechanism for SMEs, and to promote economic growth and employment via pragmatic collaboration that directly benefits people.

BRICS are anticipated to encourage pragmatic collaboration for e-commerce growth and support the development of e-commerce SME with an open, unified, inclusive, and cooperative attitude. It is anticipated to continue to expand and improve the BRIC e-commerce development cooperation mechanism, with the goal of maintaining economic and job growth. BRIC nations use their complementary resource endowment and industrial structure to expand field collaboration and create a multi-field, multi-level, and all-around cooperation pattern. Today, the BRICS nations have developed over 60 instruments of collaboration, including an e-commerce cooperation framework. The implementation and driving power of the BRICS governments are critical factors in promoting in-depth collaboration in important sectors. To accomplish the BRICS national objectives, we must continuously enhance the BRICS e-commerce development system.

Although significant progress has been made, the issues must not be overlooked. The interests and views of various nations vary, especially when it comes to certain cooperative issues, which has an impact on cooperation and promotion to some extent. BRICS members must improve their e-commerce cooperation consensus in order to genuinely boost e-commerce cooperation and achieve significant economic success for BRICS SMEs. The growth of e-commerce is not only linked to the growth of e-commerce businesses, but it is also linked to the growth of SMEs. The sector of e-commerce, as a major area of cooperation and one of the BRICS nations' main objectives, has a significant driving force. As a result, the BRICS nations should prioritise strategic positioning in order to minimise disparities and commit to fostering a win-win, healthy, and fast e-commerce growth. Under the current cooperation framework, the BRICS must also encourage strategic planning that is favourable to e-commerce collaboration and growth. The government's strategic planning has a direct effect on the degree of e-commerce development. E-commerce should be taken into consideration and given a prominent role in national planning as a major area of cooperation for the BRICS nations. Governments should adhere to inclusive and win-win cooperation in order to promote deep cooperation.

Effective implementation is one of the most important aspects of a cooperative mechanism's efficacy. To balance the rights and responsibilities of different parties and ensure the effectiveness of BRICS cooperation, BRICS countries must overcome the problems and shortcomings of previous cooperation processes and seek to establish a framework of mutual recognition, equality, and mutual benefit, clear powers, mutual restraint, stable and predictable rules system.

To begin, all parties must agree on the norms and regulations for expanding cooperative strategic investment, which includes people, money, facilities, cooperative initiatives, and system design.

Second, establish clear short- and long-term cooperation goals and benefit-sharing rules, as well as safeguards, evaluation, supervision, rewards and punishments, and a dispute-resolution mechanism, to avoid the impact of collaboration efficiency on the declaration of cooperation due to a lack of strict evaluation.

Third, fully use the government of various countries' strategic advice and institutional guarantees to ensure that the BRICS nations' e-commerce cooperation is stable and orderly.

Fourth, make full use of international bodies to coordinate BRICS e-commerce cooperation promotion. In recent years, the BRICS countries have coordinated their positions and spoken with a single voice with other major international organisations such as the United Nations, the Group of Twenty (G20), the World Trade Organization

(WTO), the International Monetary Fund (IMF), and the World Bank on a variety of global governance and other major issues (WB). The United Nations Industrial Development Organization (UNIDO), the World Trade Organization (WTO), the World Bank, and other international organisations have all undertaken e-commerce-related initiatives and projects (see Table 6.1). To boost BRICS nations' e-commerce cooperation, the group must continue to fully support the role of international organisations, enhance BRICS SMEs' collaboration via e-commerce development, and expedite the achievement of the 2030 Sustainable Development Agenda objectives. Furthermore, as stated in the Goa Declaration of the BRICS National Leaders' eighth meeting, "close cooperation between the BRICS countries in various fields, the Economic and Trade Liaison Group, the Business Council, the New Development Bank, and the Interbank Cooperation Mechanism" is critical to the BRICS economic and trade partnership's strengthening.

BRICS countries can fully develop their comparative advantages and support enterprises to cooperate in cross-border, regional, and sub-regional information and communication networks by promoting market cooperation of BRICS communication networks, particularly in the areas of 3G, 4G, and 5G communication networks and telecommunication broadband network development, database development, and big data platform sharing.

he capacity of logistics and distribution infrastructure is the second area of emphasis. One of the most frequent issues confronting the global growth of e-commerce is the degree of logistical infrastructure and distribution capacity, which has a direct impact on and defines the amount of e-commerce development. The world's top e-commerce firms, Amazon and JD.com, owe their success on their strong logistics and distribution networks. Alibaba's own logistics system, Cainiao, has also improved in recent years. To achieve mutual benefit and win-win development, the rapid development of e-commerce in BRICS countries requires a focus on and strengthening the supply capacity of logistics and distribution infrastructure, as well as active cooperation between logistics enterprises, particularly in developed and developing areas, such as joint construction and sharing of logistics warehouse distribution centres. Strengthening transportation capacity is the third priority area. Local transportation infrastructure affects logistics and distribution capacity. Building transportation capacity, improving transportation infrastructure, and improving accessibility, convenience, and timeliness are all necessary factors for a country's and region's fast economic growth. Not only do the BRICS nations need to improve their infrastructure and capacity, but they also need to improve cross-border transportation connectivity cooperation. The creation of a BRICS railway research network, for example, is now being discussed. This seeks to encourage railway research and development in order to achieve cost-effective and long-term economic growth.

The World Economic Forum's research shows that the state cannot rely solely on the development of information infrastructure to improve competitiveness; only by implementing a comprehensive modernization infrastructure strategy for technology protection, innovation, and enterprise development can the benefits of information communication technology be fully realised. As a result, technology-related e-commerce development requires a lot of creativity and collaboration. Scientific and technical innovation collaboration has previously been carried out within the framework of BRICS cooperation, and working mechanisms such as BRICS ministerial meetings, senior officials' meetings, and working group meetings have been created. The BRICS nations formed a working group on scientific and technological innovation funding in 2016, and signed the "BRICS Science and Technological Innovation Framework Programme" and "Implementation Plan." The BRICS countries have collaborated on ten scientific and technological innovation projects, including disaster management, water and pollution control, geospatial technology and its applications, new energy, renewable energy, and energy efficiency, astronomy, biological technology and biological medicine (including human health and neuroscience), information technology, and astronomy. On this premise, BRICS should expand and deepen their collaboration in the area of technical support for e-commerce development, in order to improve the level of technical support and service in BRICS e-commerce.

E-commerce growth in BRICS nations need a competent and trained staff. Following the fast growth of e-commerce in the BRICS nations, governments must improve training and collaboration in order to create multi-skilled workers. BRICS nations should strive to improve the ease of personal interaction and communication among member countries within the current cooperation framework (especially skilled and professional e-commerce staff). International organisations must be fully used to carry out advanced staff training and exchanges in the field of e-commerce. BRICS nations and businesses may acquire a better knowledge of each other's ecosystems by undertaking joint research on e-commerce trends, frontier technologies, and shared issues, for example. The fast growth of e-commerce may be aided by strengthening the interchange and collaboration among the BRICS industry organisations.

Cooperation with local e-commerce businesses and platforms, particularly in cross-border payment, logistics, customs clearance, after-sales, and other sectors, must be enhanced in order to expand e-commerce penetration in target nations and regions. It is feasible to constantly enhance the shopping experience of consumers via the integration of globalisation and localization alone, thus promoting the fast growth of cross-border e-commerce.

Varied nations have different data management, consumer rights protection, and internet information access laws, all of which have hampered cross-border commerce. These restrictions have not only established new market barriers, but they have also raised the cost of entry into the global market for SMEs. The ability to transmit information and data across the board in a free and efficient way without the limitations of technological hurdles or anti-competitive bottlenecks is a requirement for success in the e-commerce industry.

One of the primary goals of the BRICS e-commerce collaboration is to stimulate and support the development of SMEs, which will lead to increased economic and employment growth (see the second part of this report). The promotion of collaboration and growth of SMEs in BRICS has a bright future in light of the fast expansion of e-commerce and the Strategic Framework of the BRICS Economic Partnership. The key to promoting BRICS SMEs' collaboration and growth is to remove market and institutional obstacles, as well as to lower SMEs' market entrance costs, market operating costs, and the costs of participating in the global economy.

Because of their small size, SMEs are particularly sensitive to logistics and distribution expenses. As a result, strengthening strategic cooperation in logistics and distribution infrastructure capabilities, as well as providing more sharing services for SMEs, can not only lower operational costs, but also improve SMEs‘ efficiency via the Internet, which is a better channel for participating in global economic development.

More SMEs have gained the ability to engage in global value chains and promote inclusive economic and social development as a result of e-commerce. Small, medium, and micro businesses provide a huge number of jobs at a cheap cost of capital, as well as self-employment possibilities in rural and undeveloped regions. Small and medium-sized businesses (SME) development via e-commerce provides employment and income to a significant number of disadvantaged populations, supporting a balanced and equitable distribution of wealth at the national and global levels.

Conclusion

The Indian retail industry is one of the most promising and thriving in the world. Multinational corporations have seen digitization as one of the paths to success because to the enormous economic possibilities. E-commerce is the greatest example of a company that has used information technology to its maximum potential. However, there are a few real issues with India's digitization approach. On the one hand, corporations gain in terms of sales and revenue, but mergers and acquisitions pose a significant danger to small and start-up businesses. As a result, there is a need to maximise the benefits of digitization while also safeguarding the interests of industry participants.

The intentional fulfilment of social duty by e-commerce platforms is insufficient. There is a lot of unpredictability, and there isn't much strategic preparation. The platform is obsessed with pursuing economic goals. Continue to prioritise users as the platform's main objective in order to draw attention. To achieve profit returns, at the cost of users, consumer interests, and societal interests. Part of the platform's reputation is poor since it employs low-cost and deceptive sales tactics, making it difficult for customers to differentiate between product quality. Most e-commerce platforms do not yet have their own self-discipline system in place, and they behave haphazardly when it comes to social responsibility. They don't have a comprehensive plan or strategy for carrying out their social responsibilities. For example, in order to preserve the environment, an e-commerce platform must make it obvious how to address the issue of excessive packing and pollution sources produced by packaging. Ordering goods via an e-commerce site generates boxes, tape, foam pads, and other packaging, all of which contribute to pollution. They are not recycled or recycled because the majority of them are non-biodegradable materials.

The intentional fulfilment of social duty by e-commerce platforms is insufficient. There is a lot of unpredictability, and there isn't much strategic preparation. The platform is obsessed with pursuing economic goals. Continue to prioritise users as the platform's main objective in order to draw attention. To achieve profit returns, at the cost of users, consumer interests, and societal interests. Part of the platform's reputation is poor since it employs low-cost and deceptive sales tactics, causing customers to be unable to differentiate between product quality. Most e-commerce platforms do not yet have their own self-discipline system in place, and they behave haphazardly when it comes to social responsibility. They don't have a comprehensive plan or strategy for carrying out their social responsibilities. For example, in order to preserve the environment, an e-commerce platform must make it obvious how to address the issue of excessive packing and pollution sources produced by packaging. Ordering goods via an e-commerce site generates boxes, tape, foam pads, and other packaging, all of which contribute to pollution. They are not recycled or recycled because the majority of them are non-biodegradable materials.

Although the government promotes e-commerce platforms that fulfil social responsibility, publicity alone is insufficient; there is no systematic legal requirement, and no proper strategy and structure to support e-commerce platforms that fulfil social duty. For a long time, the government has focused on e-commerce platforms' earnings and taxes, as well as economic growth and local accomplishments, as well as the absence of oversight and enforcement of problems like workers' rights and interests and environmental protection on e-commerce platforms. The link between e-commerce platform growth and the long-term development of the local economy and environmental protection is disregarded, and e-commerce platform oversight is undermined. Although the government encourages e-commerce platforms to freely and completely implement social responsibility, no preferential measures have been implemented to offer e-commerce platforms that actively fulfil social duty with different property and non-property interests.

The absence of social monitoring is the most serious issue that has to be addressed in order to enhance the e-commerce platform's social responsibility. A broad variety of social levels are involved in social monitoring. Because the government and the mainstream media do not properly advertise, do not completely comprehend public opinion's direction, and do not do enough to broadcast the experience of social responsibility, the general public lacks knowledge of social responsibility. They just believe that the e-commerce platform's social duty is to pay taxes and generate jobs, and that they should also contribute to society. The mass monitoring of the social responsibility e-commerce platform has not been set up, the reporting mechanism has not been created, and the informant has not been protected or rewarded after reporting. As a result, when social responsibility incidents occur on e-commerce platforms, the general public is often unable to actively report to the appropriate authorities in a timely manner.

The modern e-commerce platform is more concerned with the timeliness of product or service information, and it also performs well in the process management of information gateways. However, the e-commerce platform's duty in terms of information creation is inadequate, owing to a lack of information originality and a lack of infringement control. The substance of information is many and varied in the age of big data. If an e-commerce platform focuses only on reproducing and reprocessing current data, it will certainly raise the user's cognitive load and increase the time it takes for the user to acquire useful information, which is the situation when consumers are bombarded with garbage data. Many e-commerce systems place too much emphasis on heat behaviour, which has exacerbated the lack of tort control to some degree. Currently, there are numerous loopholes in the regulation and limitation of violation of intellectual property, copyright, and personal privacy in different nations' legal systems, resulting in the occurrence of e-commerce platform domain torts on occasion.

The present e-commerce platform is more skewed towards the conventional retail industry's customer rights and interests, disregarding the online nature of the purchasing platform, which is expressed via language or text. Symbols, such as images, convey cultural meanings. The e-commerce platform's network consumption culture is defined by terms like "cost-effective and easy," "usage and satisfaction," "fun," and so on. The line between the actual world and the virtual world is becoming more blurred as a consequence of such consuming culture, resulting in contradictions and conflicts such as social consumption level gaps, aberrant advertising, excessive consumption, and so on.

The social responsibility report of an e-commerce platform should be promoted and enhanced in the future, including disclosing the status of social responsibility, preparing measures, and enhancing communication ways and discussion mechanisms. Keep up with and react to the opinions of stakeholders. Encourage the whole industry to acquire a sense of social responsibility. Simultaneously, it is necessary to continue to improve the platform's alignment with international practises and standards, to disseminate information, to bind their own business activities to international social responsibility standards, and to introduce independent third-party assessments to increase authority and credibility.

Harmonious labour relations are critical for maintaining social stability and the healthy growth of e-commerce businesses. Both parties of a labour dispute must fulfil their responsibilities while exercising their rights. Regardless of whether the labour connection is established via a labour contract or a non-labor relationship through a commercial contract, all parties have the right to legal protection.

In the evolution of the road, e-commerce platforms have grown more mobile, social, intelligent, and customised. This makes the e-commerce platform's ecological environment more varied and complicated, resulting in a slew of new issues and circumstances. E-commerce platforms' social responsibility is becoming more important, and it will be the emphasis in the future. The e-commerce platform has caused a slew of issues; all we can do now is attempt to minimise the negative impacts of these platforms using scientific techniques. We may face extremely serious repercussions if we do not act now.

[1] Noshir Kaka, Anu Madgavkar, Alok Kshirsagar, Rajat Gupta, James Manyika, KusheBahl, and Shishir Gupta, *Digital India: Technology to Transform a Connected Nation*, McKinsey Global Institute (Mar., 2019).

[2] Ravi Seetaramaraju and Krishna Diatha, *Adoption of Digital Payments by Small Retail Stores*, ACIS 2018 Proceedings, 41 (2018).

[3] riyanka Singh, Gursimranjit Singh, and Maninder Singh, *Let's Get Phygital: M-Commerce as a Crusader for "Phygital" Retail*, in M-Commerce: Experiencing the Phygital Retail, ed. Punita Duhan and Anurag Singh (New York: Apple Academic Press, 2019), 145 – 162.

[4] Ministry of Commerce of the PRC, *13th Five-Year* Planning for the Development of e-commerce, available at: http://images.mofcom.gov.cn/dzsws/201612/20161229191628547.pdf

[5] Turban E., Outland J., King D., Lee J.K., Liang TP., Turban D.C., *E-Commerce: Regulatory, Ethical, and Social Environments*. In: Electronic Commerce 2018. Springer Texts in Business and Economics. Springer, Cham (2018).

[6] Kumar, V., *A study of E-commerce and its legal frame work: With special reference to India* (2017).

[7]*Supra Note* 5

[8] Alexander Pons, *Global e-commerce: a framework for understanding and overcoming the trust barrier*, Information Management & Computer Security, Vol. 11, Issue. 3, pp.130-138 (2003).

[9] Dieter Fink, *Value decomposition of e-commerce performance*, Benchmarking: An International Journal, Vol. 13 Issue. 1/2, pp. 81 -92 (2006).

[10] Xue, Yan, Cheng Ouyang, Hongjie Wan, and Zhengwei Jiang, *Future of Global Trade: Connecting the World Through E-commerce*, Alibaba Research Institute, Ali Cross-border E-commerce Research Center, 2016. Web. 3 July 2017.

[11] Sharma, Chandru, *The Future of Ecommerce - Further Thinking around Ecommerce, Ecommerce Guide*, (Jun. 13, 2017), available at: https://ecommerceguide.com/guides/ecommerce-future/.

[12] Gilder, George, *Making Business Sense of the Internet*, Harvard Business Review (Mar.-Apr., 1994).

[13] Nerurkar, A., *Online Marketing - Challenges In Future*, IMPACT: International Journal of Research in Humanities, Arts and Literature ,Vol. 2, Issue 4, Apr 2014, pp. 183-188 (2014).

[14] Soni, V. & Pandey, B.B., *Impact of Digitalization in E-Marketing*, International Journal for Innovative Research in Science & Technology, ISSN (online): 2349-6010, Volume 3, Issue 05, p. 120 (2016).

[15] Shivasankaran, S., *Digital Marketing and Its Impact on Buying Behavior of Youth* (Special Reference to Kanyakumari District), International Journal of Research in

Management & Business Studies , Vol. 4 Issue 3, (SPL 1), pp. 35-39 (2017).

[16] Satadruti Chakraborty, and Dipa Mitra, *A Study on Consumers' Adoption Intention For Digital Wallets In India*, International Journal on Customer Relations, 6, no. 1, pp. 38–57 (2018).

[17] Amitkumar L Shah, *An Analysis of the Technology Acceptance Model in Understanding Retailers Behavioural Intention to Use Paytm – A Digitalwallet*, Journal of Management & Research, 8 no, 1, pp. 78–84 (2018).

[18]*Supra Note* 12

[19]*Id.*

[20] E. Brynjolfsson, Y.J. Hu, M.S. Rahman, *Competing in the age of omni-channel retailing*, MIT Sloan Management Review, 54(4), pp. 23-29 (2013).

[21] K. Clarke, R.W. Belk, *The effects of product involvement and task definition on anticipated consumer effort*, Wilkie, W. L. (Ed.) NA – Advances in Consumer Research, 6 , pp. 313-318 (1979).

[22] P.K. Kannan, A. Li, *Digital marketing: A framework, review and research agenda*, International Journal of Research in Marketing, 34 (1), pp. 22-45 (2017).

[23] J.-C. Kim, S.H. Chun, *Cannibalization and competition effects of a manufacturer's retail channel strategies: Implications on an omni-channel business model*, Decision Support Systems, 109, pp. 5-14 (2018).

[24]*Id.*

[25]*Supra Note* 22.

[26] Van Welie, Richard, Jorij Abraham, and Roald Willemsen, *Brazil B2C E-commerce Report* (2016).

[27] Rinck, Edvard, Michael KK Ma, and Lilly Cheung, *E-commerce strategy and must-haves in China* (2015).

[28] Howland, Daphne, *E-commerce in India: The opportunities and the obstacles*, Retail Dive. Industry Dive (Apr. 5, 2016).

[29] Xue, Yan, Cheng Ouyang, Hongjie Wan, and Zhengwei Jiang, *Future of Global Trade: Connecting the World Through E-commerce*, Ali Cross-border E-commerce Research Center (2016).

CHAPTER FIVE

CONFIDENTIALITY IN ONLINE ARBITRATIONS: SHORTCOMINGS IN THE INDIAN POSITION AND THE WAY FORWARD

Background

It is vital to grasp the social element of arbitration hearings in order to appreciate the need of confidentiality in any arbitration procedure. Data confidentiality is one of the most sought after advantages that arbitration delivers to the parties, amongst the mentioned list of advantages that arbitration has to give, ranging from fast, effective, and flexibility of the process. Owing to the COVID-19 pandemic, and arbitration hearings taking a virtual route, it becomes imperative to ensure extension of the protection of confidentiality to virtual hearings in order to safeguard personalised data such as login credentials of an individual, as well as documentation for such hearings saved by companies and firms, both coming under the category of firms. Such protection can hence be extended vis-à-vis the recognition of the right to privacy of such person, as the same becomes a basis to call for application of the relevant data protection statutes, ensuring a legitimate basis to claim security of the data thereinafter.

Typically, parties request protection for papers containing trade secrets or other sensitive commercial information. To avoid such disclosure of their personal information, it has been seen that the number of parties who choose Arbitration as their dispute resolution process has outnumbered those who prefer ordinary legal proceedings.

The Arbitration and Conciliation (Amendment) Act, 2019, introduced confidentiality in arbitration for the first time in India. The goal of this Amendment Act was to turn India into a centre for domestic and international arbitration. However, there is still a lot of uncertainty about data confidentiality, and arbitral institutions may be able to help in these situations by assuring stronger compliance and creating solid data security protocols.

The authors attempt to bring about the need and means for legislative inclusivity of confidentiality in arbitration in this article. The article, through methodological triangulation (doctrinal approach) identifies data protection practical needs and legal challenges in virtual arbitrations, following which through a reform oriented approach, provides a detailed insight into the legal means and need to tackle the issue of breach of confidentiality in virtual arbitrations in India through a critical examination of the existing legal position in India, indicating a way forward.

Introduction

The rise in the use of virtual hearings in arbitration processes has been attributed to the adoption of COVID-19 and the constraints it has prompted. Arbitral institutions around the world reacted quickly, issuing protocols and guidelines and hosting webinars to regulate and discuss this unique type of hearing, highlighting the similarities and differences between it and “ordinary” ones. The preceding situation highlighted a number of issues, including whether and how the requirement for confidentiality in arbitration (with a focus on commercial arbitration) can be protected when virtual hearings are used.

Confidentiality, among other issues, is a big deal breaker, making Arbitration a realistic option. For a long time, confidentiality in arbitration has been the subject of several arguments and disputes. The main challenge is whether or not arbitral procedures can comply with the system's confidentiality requirements. There are still lingering doubts about the scope and enforceability of confidentiality agreements. Due to a recent development in which arbitration is being moved to an online platform, the uncertainty associated with respecting the confidentiality clause in arbitration has become even hazier. This exacerbates the issue and creates its own set of problems.

Confidentiality in an arbitration case means that all proceedings in any session of international commercial arbitration will be conducted in camera, and that the arbitral award will not be released in the public domain without both parties‘ prior approval. There are two types of confidentiality: (a) confidentiality between the parties as a result of the obligation imposed on them, and (b) confidentiality with respect to the substance of the proceeding, which includes documents, hearings, and other evidence.[1]

The principle of confidentiality has always clashed with that of public interest, as well as other ideals such as mandatory disclosures to some stakeholders in a dispute, such as shareholders or insurers, when an arbitral award is challenged in court. Among the numerous benefits of confidentiality are the avoidance of unfavourable legal precedents and the reduction of the risk of compromising ongoing commercial relationships.

In general, the level of confidentiality in arbitration will vary based on a number of criteria. As a result, the effect of virtual hearings on confidentially must be assessed on a case-by-case basis rather than in broad terms. This is directly related to the ambiguity surrounding the definition of confidentiality in arbitration in the first place. While it is widely accepted that confidentiality should be imposed on the parties, the arbitral tribunal, and any arbitration institution present when applicable, whether the same should be imposed on third parties who may participate in the proceedings (such as experts or witnesses) is unclear.

When in the wrong hands, technology might jeopardise the integrity of the arbitral process. It is important to understand that all proceedings, whether online or offline, are held with the sole purpose of providing both parties with a private setting in which they can settle their disputes without fear of information being leaked.[2] It's crucial to know what technologies are being employed and to what degree they're being utilised for this. Video conferencing, emails, and file management systems are among the technologies used in online arbitration. There's also the idea of electronic filing and case management. It's tough to restrict the spread of information once it's on the internet.

There are certain actors and authorities that bear responsibility for data transmission under the international commercial framework. This is now a critical point to consider because, in the presence of various jurisdictional regimes, data transfer via online platform across borders in the presence of complicated technology becomes quite risky. With multiple layers of data transfer and high penalties for violating data protection laws, a robust and standard data protection framework is required.

Data Confidentiality and associated concerns

As a consequence of the internet's never-ending expansion, several professions and service providers have carved out a niche for themselves. The internet's development has had an impact on many facets of human existence, including regulation. The internet cleared the path for digital networking and the global e-expansion markets. The way material is handled, as well as copyright and press restrictions, has changed as a result of this. Because the internet's dynamism leads to greater international and domestic commerce, it's critical to think about how to modernise out-of-court dispute settlement. Every economy has been compelled to shutter its doors due to the present conditions put on the world economy by the COVID-19 epidemic. Not only does an individual lose a considerable amount of money, but the economy as a whole also suffers. Despite the fact that the situation has not improved, efforts are being made to resuscitate the economy in whatever manner possible. Introducing economic generators to online channels is a significant step forward in this direction.

On the other hand, the ODR mechanism was not a satisfactory success.[3] Firstly, various hardware limitations have rendered the ODR unavailable to a large segment of the population. The data prices in India are the lowest in the world; for example, in the United States, a GB of data costs INR 592, but in India, it costs just INR. 7. However, supplying low-cost data does not imply that the equipment necessary to use it are easily available. As a result, a lack of infrastructure and access to computer resources is creating a significant impediment to the growth of ODR.

The second factor is user awareness. Users' knowledge of technology and digital literacy is among the lowest among internet users worldwide. More than 90% of Indians (see here) are unaware of the extent and correct use of the internet and technology, and are fully reliant on the younger generation for even the most basic Facebook and WhatsApp setup. As a result, people's lack of understanding and mental barriers must be addressed and enhanced in order for it to be accessible to the general public.

The third issue is a scarcity of qualified specialists. Despite the fact that 10% of the Indian population is deemed digitally literate, this literacy is mostly found in the informal sector. However, India's courts and justice system work on a procedural basis, and moving them to a new platform need a well-trained and enhanced support structure. Only until the justice support system has been educated will they be able to go farther in informing people about ODR and other online court mechanisms.

Finally, one of the most important reasons is the high upfront cost of implementing approved technology, as well as the ongoing risk of data loss and device hacking. Due to the existence of aforementioned issues, the parties were discouraged from employing ODR.[4]

On the other hand, Confidentiality of proceedings indubitably remains one of the prime advantages of Arbitration. Traditionally, confidentiality would entail the protection from public disclosure of what takes place during the Arbitration.[5] The premise is to protect the interest of parties that often have to rely on critical commercial information such as profit margins, pricing policies, know-how or trade secrets etc. and other sensitive data that might potentially impact their overall public image to make their case in a proceeding.

It has widely been debated if confidentiality forms the bedrock of an arbitration proceeding. Confidentiality is affected by the parties' choice of rules governing the arbitration and also the choice of place of arbitration. Some rules tend to be more predisposed towards confidentiality requirements whereas others may not treat confidentiality as a vital requirement of the arbitration clause. Some jurisdictions, such as the United States of America, Sweden and Australia, do not treat confidentiality as an inherent part of the arbitration and hence, in absence of any explicit agreement to that effect, the parties' are not usually duty bound by any confidentiality obligation.[6] However, in jurisdictions such as the United Kingdom, confidentiality is treated as an implicit feature of the arbitration clause.[7] Therefore, even in the absence of express requirements for confidentiality there is a general obligation on the parties to maintain confidentiality of the proceedings.

It can nevertheless be said that the parties enjoy sufficient autonomy in arbitration to meticulously choose the set of laws that would favour their requirement for confidentiality. However, in the face of increasing virtualization of the proceedings, especially in the wake of the Covid-19 pandemic, it is imperative to analyze how well equipped are the existing laws to tackle the new dimensions of privacy and confidentiality that have emerged with this virtualization.

The word 'technology' clearly dominates the term 'online arbitration'. In the wrong hands, technology will jeopardise the integrity of the arbitral process. It is important to note that all hearings, whether online or offline, are conducted for the express purpose of providing all sides with a confidential setting in which they can resolve their differences without the risk of information being leaked. It's crucial to know what tools are being used and to what degree they're being used for this. Video conferencing, emails, and file management applications are among the technologies used in online arbitration. Another option is that of electronic records, which was suggested by the 2017 High-Level committee chaired by Justice B.N. Srikrishna (Retired) under Section 43K of the Act. However, Section 43K of the Arbitration Act empowers the Arbitration Council of India to keep an electronic depository of arbitral awards and other associated records in the manner provided by the rules. Once it is notified and rules are developed, it will be fascinating to examine how Section 42A, which provides for secrecy, interacts with Section 43K, which provides for depository. In order to guarantee confidentiality, the Committee advised that only Courts have access to the repository for the restricted purpose of viewing the arbitral award. This proposal, however, was rejected, and there is no mention of it in Section 43K.

According to a report released by Logic Force[8], a cybersecurity consultancy company, large corporations have been targeted by hackers. Despite the fact that they are at risk of serious publicity, most law firms are not well trained to deal with these dangers. Arbitrators and Arbitral institutions are particularly vulnerable to cybersecurity threats because they store confidential data. An instance can be the hacking of the Permanent Court of Arbitration in 2015[9], during a hearing of a sensitive maritime boundary dispute between China and the Philippines. Lastly, arbitrations may also include parties that are leading targets of cybersecurity threats, such as multinational corporations, governments or state bodies, public figures, and/or non-governmental organisations (NGOs). International arbitration cases also include verification of proof that are not available in the public domain but have the ability to affect politics and capital markets.

There are specific actors and officials who assume responsibility for data transmission under the international commercial system. This is now a critical point to remember because, in the presence of various jurisdictional regimes, data transmission via online portal across borders in the presence of complicated technologies becomes very dangerous.[10] With several layers of data transfer and high penalties for violating data privacy laws, a stable and standard data protection system is needed.

The legal status quo in India

India recently took efforts to guarantee that people's privacy is respected. In 2017, the country's Supreme Court made history by affirming the right to privacy as a fundamental right in the Puttaswamy Case[11]. Because this decision was a watershed moment in India's advancement of privacy laws, it's important to understand the timeline. During this time, the Indian government formed an expert committee led by Justice B.N. Srikrishna to develop a data security policy for the region, which eventually led to the Personal Data Protection Bill Draft. Long before this Bill was introduced in 2017, the Indian government established another committee, chaired by Justice BN Srikrishna, to review various issues related to data security in India and make clear recommendations on the standards that will underpin a Data Protection Bill.

The Personal Data Protection Bill, 2019 (hereinafter "PDP")[12] aims to regulate data privacy in India and abroad by granting territoriality to companies with a commercial relationship with India or who conduct such profiling of individuals in India. PDP refers to all sorts of personal data and is classified into two categories: sensitive and essential. Because the General Data Protection Regulation (hereinafter "GDPR")[13], a robust framework regulating data exchange and disclosure in the European Union, fails to expressly help us understand how data protection issues in other fields of law will be handled, arbitration fails to expressly help us understand how data confidentiality issues in other fields of law will be handled. The judicial system, like any other constitutionally protected entitlement, may be abused. Some fear that enacting/tightening data protection legislation may open up new avenues for "frivolous" legal action from unscrupulous parties, which might cost businesses a lot of time and money. Due to a lack of bipartisan consensus and cooperation among legislators, data privacy bills are frequently "gutted" / "watered down" by the time they are passed into law, failing to sufficiently safeguard consumer privacy rights (but still costs corporations time and money and imposes limitations of how they operate). The many personal information privacy standards imposed by separate states might impose additional constraints on businesses without a simplified federal statute. Furthermore, having each state establish its own personal data protection legislation creates the risk of conflict between state standards, making lawful data exchange difficult or impossible. ODR institutions must spend in compliance training, install new data management equipment, and maybe hire extra staff and evaluators to become/stay compliant with data protection and privacy regulations, incurring expenditures they did not have previously.

Non-personal information is exempt from the GDPR, which specifies that disclosure of personal information may be justified for reasons such as consumer protection, public safety, law enforcement, rights enforcement, cybersecurity, and fraud prevention. Furthermore, the GDPR does not apply to domain names registered by American registrars and registries for US registrants. It also doesn't apply to domain name registrants who aren't "natural people," such as organisations, businesses, or other legal entities. Despite this, because the GDPR's rules are so unclear and the possible penalties are so significant, parties such as ICANN use voluntary filtering. Proponents of the GDPR are likely to have contributed to the perception that the GDPR encourages procedures like the Temporary Specification.

Without effective measures to foster education or innovation, the GDPR and CCPA maintain the status quo, rewarding the largest players while punishing small and medium-sized businesses and deceiving individuals into believing they have better privacy when they are really being placed at danger. The bureaucratization of data protection does not result in the creation of a natural right to privacy. Having an ever-increasing number of regulators and rules governing data does not make a person safer. Regulation maintains the status quo; it does not promote system or user knowledge development.

The GDPR has a significant unintended consequence of undermining the transparency of the international mechanisms and architecture that manage the internet. The Internet Corporation for Assigned Names and Numbers (ICANN) has published a Temporary Specification that permits registries and registrars to suppress WHOIS data that was previously needed to be made public, presumably to comply with the GDPR. This might stymie attempts to tackle illegal activities online, such as identity theft, cyberattacks, online espionage, intellectual property theft, fraud, illegal drug sales, human trafficking, and other crimes, and it isn't even required under the GDPR.

This may have given you a hint that India currently lacks data privacy regulations, let alone a specialised arbitration code. The 1996 Arbitration and Conciliation Act, as important as it is for party control and confidentiality, is plagued by statutory issues. Despite the fact that the Act was updated to include Sections 42A and 43K, the public has yet to be notified. As a consequence, there is a great deal of uncertainty regarding how data security and, by extension, confidentiality may be addressed in the arbitral procedures now underway in India.

The non-obstante provision in Section 42A of the amended Act states that all parties in the trials must maintain confidentiality, with the exception of the prize, which must be disclosed if the award is to be enforced and implemented. The rights of any party desiring to bring sensitive material from arbitration to a court are now in doubt as a result of this statute.

The law dealing to Confidentiality Clubs has been characterised by constantly shifting jurisprudence over the last few years. Given that only the Delhi High Court has established some conditions for their formation and that there is no statutory provision to recognise these clubs, it has become more of an emerging judge-made legislation.

A detailed examination of the above-mentioned passed orders reveals that the membership of Confidentiality Clubs is still unclear. The *Transformative Learning Solutions*[14]and *Genentech Inc.* [15]orders, which enable the inclusion of parties and internal experts, differ from previous orders that only permitted advocates and external experts to be members of the clubs. It would be interesting to observe how the courts create these groups in the future to safeguard the secret of the records.

The constitution of these clubs is expected to be expanded in the coming days to include litigation in other areas such as arbitration, competition law, and data protection. Given the prevalence of these clubs in court processes, having a structured, controlled statutory framework becomes vitally crucial. Given that this is one of the exceptions to the open justice principles, a framework is required to strike a compromise between preserving sensitive information and ensuring open justice access.

Another important factor to consider is the participation of other parties in the arbitral process, which may be reliant on sensitive material discovered during the arbitration in cases of consolidation of multiple arbitral proceedings or joinder of parties to an initiated or ongoing arbitration.

In Vidya Drolia and Ors. v. Durga Trading Corporation[16], the Supreme Court of India allowed third parties to assert their reference in arbitration proceedings by demonstrating their level of interest, implying that such reference proceedings may necessitate the disclosure of sensitive arbitration details. The Court delved deeper into the issue of subject-matter arbitrability and the scope and ambit of the Court's jurisdiction while dealing with an application made under Section 8 or 11 of the Arbitration and Conciliation Act, 1996, while dealing with an application made under Section 8 or 11 of the TPA.

As a consequence, Indian courts will need to specify the criteria for releasing sensitive information in court proceedings, as well as consider the interests of parties seeking an exemption under Section 42A of the Act. Other nations, such as Singapore and the United Kingdom, are currently debating this legal problem. The conflict of interest that arises when providing information for the public good persists; however, since the public good is an exception to the clause, a balancing method is necessary. One of the aims of the Arbitration and Conciliation (Amendment) Act, 2019 (hereinafter "2019 Amendment")[17] was to create the Arbitration Council of India as an autonomous regulatory body for all arbitrations held in India. It also wants the Arbitration Council of India (hereinafter "ACI") to settle on data fiduciaries and data principles as part of the PDP Bill. Since the PDP bill determines what a data fiduciary is, it is unclear whether the data fiduciary is an arbitrator or an arbitral institution. Even while such provisions try to protect data security, they fall short of solving the situation at hand, hence India demands a data privacy protocol immediately.

Shaping Indian Arbitral Institutions: A lesson from International Arbitral Institutions

Institutional Arbitrations have always stood as a tall example of ensuring uniformity and providing a definite structure for arbitration proceedings through their own set of rules. These rules usually provide flexibility with regard to the procedural measures to be adopted in the smooth conduction of arbitral proceeding.[18] They have especially stood out in the Covid times because of their quick adaptability and ability to handle virtual hearings and e-filings.

Despite the new challenges faced in terms of security and confidentiality, arbitral institutions have been producing guidance to best address these challenges. Best practices would see parties, their representatives and the arbitrator agreeing on a set of reasonable precautions to be taken with regard to cybersecurity, privacy and data protection at the start of arbitration proceedings to ensure an appropriate level of security for the case.

Institutionalization of arbitration in India is still at a budding stage and the need to strengthen Institutional Arbitration in India has acquired more relevance than ever due to the restrictions posed by the pandemic. The Amendment Act, 2019 setup the Arbitration Council of India for grading arbitral institutions with an attempt to strengthen institutional arbitration in India. Presently there are about 35 arbitral institutions in India such as the Indian Council of Arbitration ("ICA"), the Delhi International Arbitration Centre ("DIAC"), the Mumbai Centre for International Arbitration ("MCIA"), to name a few. But only a handful of them actively partake in arbitration and have continued to do so during the pandemic. There is a significant lot that India can learn from the international institutional practice in terms of fortifying its infrastructure to accommodate the need of the hour.

Some of the international institutional rules already provided a mechanism for remote hearing and aid of digital support for conducting arbitration even before this pandemic induced digital revolution was brought about in the realm of Arbitration. For instance, the Hong Kong International Arbitration Centre (HKIAC) had introduced provisions centered on the use of technology for document submission and conduction of arbitration proceeding three years ago in 2018.[19] The International Chamber of Commerce ("ICC") too already provided for the 'use of telephone or video conferencing for procedural and other hearings where attendance in person is not essential and use of virtual tools that enables online communication among the parties, the arbitral tribunal and the Secretariat of the Court.'[20] In fact, Rule 24(4) of the ICC Rules also provides that the case management conference may be held virtually over telephone or video call.

Others seem to have adapted to the exigent and special requirements of the current times by modelling new rules to support virtual arbitration in pandemic times. The ICC and SIAC are currently successfully facilitating arbitration proceedings involving parties located in various jurisdictions by way of video conferencing, and have released guidelines and advisories for the conduct of arbitrations in these times. The ICC released its 'Guidance Note on Possible Measures Aimed at Mitigating the Effects of the COVID-19 Pandemic' ("ICC COVID19 Guidance") in April 2020.[21] SIAC, on the other hand, has addressed issues pertaining to the virtual conduct of arbitration through the SIAC-COVID FAQs available on its website.[22] The CIArb released a detailed guidance note on Remote Dispute Resolution Proceedings with specific provisions on confidentiality and security.[23] In India, the Mumbai Centre for International Arbitration (MCIA) has also continued to operate virtually and provided parties with the option to conduct remote arbitrations using its audio-video capabilities.[24]

With this particular indispensability of digitization of arbitration by Institutional Rules, confidentiality has acquired a new flavour with some special issues such as data protection and cyber security that need to be addressed. The International Institute for Conflict Prevention & Resolution has recognized the paramount importance of confidentiality in virtual proceedings and has empowered the tribunal to terminate the proceedings if it feels that confidentiality is compromised during the process.[25] It also prohibits access to the live video and/ or audio feed of the proceeding other than disclosed Participants. All participants are advised to avoid the use of open or public WiFi networks and required to join through wired or secure wifi networks, which may include the use of a reliable virtual private network ("VPN").[26]

The CIArb guidance has taken meticulous care even with respect to the surroundings in which the participants shall be seated during the virtual proceeding. Article 6.3 of the guidance note requires the sound proofing of the setting where possible, and also requires the positioning of the camera in a fashion that allows sufficient visibility to eliminate the possibility of the presence of undisclosed non-participating individuals in the surrounding.[27] This addresses the concern regarding the presence of a third party in the room where the witness or expert is supposed to be giving the evidence. Other than the stipulated provisions of institutional rules, recourse shall also be taken to instruments such as the ICCA-NYC Bar-CPR Protocol on Cybersecurity in International Arbitration (2020 Edition) and the IBA Cybersecurity Guidelines 2018 to address cyber security concerns. The former particularly sets out information and cyber security risks factors in an arbitration proceeding and provides guidance in determining reasonable cyber security measures for a virtual arbitration.[28]

The Indian Institutional framework can take inspiration from the international developments in Institutional arbitration across the globe and homogenise them to prepare an appropriate mix suited for the Indian palate. In this regard, the IAF Protocol on Virtual Hearings for Arbitrations released in 2020 seems be a decent attempt at a holistic guidance on virtual proceedings.[29] It provides, inter alia, the use of end to end encrypted communication channels and networks. Special emphasis is also to data processing and storage in those servers whose location is identifiable and attracts the applicable laws. It also recommends reference to the ICCA-NYC Bar-CPR Protocol on Cybersecurity in International Arbitration for ensuring adequate cyber security measures. However, in the long run, to avoid unnecessary delays and potential disagreement over applicable rules, it is advisable that the arbitral institutes incorporate their own specific provisions in their institutional rules itself to which the parties would have subscribed while choosing the administering institution.

The Way Forward

Confidentiality under Arbitration was for the very first time introduced in India by way of The Arbitration and Conciliation (Amendment) Act, 2019. The objective behind bringing this Amendment Act was to develop India into a hub of domestic and international arbitration. No doubt that a ground breaking attempt was made by Indian Legislature by bringing Sections 42A and 43K via the 2019 Amendment. Both these provisions were introduced with the hope to the course of confidentiality under arbitration. However, the outline of Section 42A and the exception provided thereunder remains arbitrary and vague in nature. Moreover, the regulations for data security by ACI are yet to see face of the dawn.

The provision makes no mention of confidentiality requirements for a case taken to court. Furthermore, by overriding sections that are in contradiction with it, the non-obstante provision introduced to the amendment further confuses the legislation. This provision does not recognise any customary exceptions, such as "public interest" and "justice." The PDP bill, however, has no mention of arbitration and does nothing to address the gap left by COVID-19's virtual arbitrations. When it comes to personal security, things are also a little foggy, and arbitration agencies may be able to help by maintaining greater uniformity and developing stringent data privacy policies.

COVID-19 has presented a plethora of new issues, but it also provides an excellent opportunity for arbitration to consider the future of information technology and the places where the two could be linked. Virtual arbitration may become the new status quo. As a result, specialised law, such as data protection, is a necessary/unavoidable requirement of the hour. According to the publishers, PDP may be amended to contain and allude to arbitration-ruled data privacy issues.

Even existing forms of courts have been relocated to the internet portal as a result of the worldwide pandemic, and there has also been an increase in online arbitration hearings with the goal of enhancing productivity and cutting expenses. People are increasingly adopting data as a critical mode of communication as the digital economy grows at an exponential rate. India not only needs a robust mechanism to fill in the gaps in its data security procedure created by the PDP Bill, but it also has to do it as fast as feasible. The government has a legal incentive to prevent all forms of cyber-attacks and maintain improved security levels.

It is currently a legislative necessity in India to require Indian courts to specify the parameters of releasing sensitive information in court cases and to consider the needs of parties requesting an exception under Section 42A. The conflict of interest that emerges when disclosing details for the public good persists; however, because the public good is an exception to the clause, a balancing mechanism is required.

The challenges with regard to proceedings confidentiality are amplified without a proper data management policy in place. The PDP Bill makes no attempt to close these gaps. It's also unclear whether data protection measures would be judged mandatory or susceptible to voluntary consensus in consent-based ad hoc arbitrations. Although it is unclear whether such restrictions would be adopted in the near future, it is vital to emphasise cybercrime's growing threat. This could lead to huge financial losses for all parties involved, as well as jeopardise the prosecutions' credibility.

In India, it's unclear how data privacy, and thus confidentiality, will be addressed. Moving toward arbitration agencies that will maintain stronger security requirements and establish stringent data preservation protocols in order to ease the myriad problems that may arise as a result of data breaches and cyber-attacks could be the answer. The ACI's laws may include a data privacy protocol to address these concerns.

There is now a regulatory opportunity to connect the PDP Bill's data protection goals with the (to-be-drafted) norms of the ACI. On the other hand, the ambiguity surrounding Section 42A's limitations on confidentiality requirements necessitates quick court intervention.

[1] Jose Rosell, *Confidentiality and arbitration*, Croatian Arbitration Yearbook, Vol. 9 (2002).

[2] Richard C. Reuben, *Confidentiality in Arbitration: Beyond the Myth*, 54 U. Kan. L. Rev. 1255 (2006).

[3] The NITI Aayog Expert Committee on ODR, *Designing the Future of Dispute Resolution: The ODR Policy Plan for India*, NITI Aayog (October, 2021), available at: https://www.niti.gov.in/sites/default/files/2021-11/odr-report-29-11-2021.pdf.

[4]*Id.*

[5] Marlon Meza-Salas (DLA Piper), *Confidentiality in International Commercial Arbitration: Truth or Fiction?*, Kluwer Arbitration Blog (Sep. 23, 2018), available at: http://arbitrationblog.kluwerarbitration.com/2018/09/23/confidentiality-in-international-commercial-arbitration-truth-or-fiction/.

[6] Esso Australia Resources Ltd. v. Hon. Sydney James Ploughman (1995), 128 ALR 391; United States v. Panhandle Eastern Corp., 118 F.R.D. 346 (Del. 1988); Bulgarian Foreign Trade Bank Ltd v. AI Trade Finance Inc, T-1881-99, Swedish Sup Ct (2000).

[7] Ali Shipping Corp. v. Shipyard Trogir, [1998] 2 All ER 136.

[8] Logic Force Consultancy, *Annual Study on Cybersecurity* (2016), available at: https://www.logicforce.com/reports/detail/cybersecurity-q1.

[9] Jason Healey and Anni Piiparinen, *Did China Just Hack the International Court Adjudicating Its South China Sea Territorial Claims?*, The Diplomat (Oct.27, 2015) available at: https://thediplomat.com/2015/10/did-china-just-hack-the-international-court-adjudicating-its-south-china-sea-territorial-claims/.

[10] UNCTAD, *Data protection regulations and international data flows: Implications for trade and development, United Nations Publication*, UNCTAD/WEB/DTL/STICT/2016/1/iPub, available at: https://unctad.org/system/files/official-document/dtlstict2016d1_en.pdf (2016).

[11] K.S. Puttaswamy v. Union of India, (2017) 10 SCC 1.

[12] The Personal Data Protection Bill, 2019, Bill No. 373 of 2019 (India).

[13] Regulation (EU) 2016/679 of the European Parliament and of the Council, *EU General Data Protection Regulation (GDPR)* (2016).

[14] Transformative Learning Solutions Pvt. Ltd. & Ors. v. Pawajot Kaur Baweja & Ors., CS(COMM) 817/2018, IA No. 5583/2018 (u/O XXXIX R-1&2 CPC) & IA No.6193/2018 (u/S 151 CPC).

[15] Genentech Inc. and Ors. v. Drugs Controller General of India and Ors., CS(OS) 3284/2015.

[16] Vidya Drolia v. Durga Trading Corporation, 2020 SCC OnLine SC 1018.

[17] The Arbitration and Conciliation (Amendment) Act, 2019, No. 52, Acts of the Parliament, 2019 (India).

[18] Report of the High Level Committee to Review the Institutionalisation of Arbitration Mechanism in India, Department of Legal Affairs, available at: https://legalaffairs.gov.in/sites/default/files/Report-

HLC.pdf (Jul. 30, 2017).

[19] Hong Kong International Arbitration Centre, *HKIAC Administered Arbitration Rules*, 2018, Article 13.1.

[20] International Chamber of Commerce, *ICC Arbitration Rules*,2021 ,Appendix IV, available at: https://iccwbo.org/dispute-resolution-services/arbitration/rules-of-arbitration/.

[21]International Chamber of Commerce, *ICC Guidance Note on Possible Measures Aimed at Mitigating the Effects of the COVID-19 Pandemic,* 2020, available at: https://iccwbo.org/content/uploads/sites/3/2020/04/guidance-note-possible-measures-mitigating-effects-covid-19-english.pdf.

[22] SIAC Covid-FAQs, available at: https://siac.org.sg/faqs/36-featured-template/advanced-shortcodes/frequently-asked-questions-faq/657-siac-covid-19-frequently-asked-questions-faqs.

[23] Chartered Institute of Arbitrators, *Guidance Note on Remote Dispute Resolution Proceedings,* 2020, available at: https://www.ciarb.org/media/9013/remote-hearings-guidance-note_final_140420.pdf.

[24] Alok Jain, Dhruv jain, *Arbitration in the time of COVID-19*, BAR AND BENCH, (May 26, 2021, 20:08 PM), https://www.barandbench.com/columns/arbitration-in-the-time-of-covid-19 .

[25] Institute for Conflict Prevention and Resolution (CPR), *Annotated Model Procedural Order for Remote Video Arbitration Proceedings,* 2020 available at: https://www.cpradr.org/resource-center/protocols-guidelines/model-procedure-order-remote-video-arbitration-proceedings.

[26]*Annotated Model Procedural Order for Remote Video Arbitration Proceedings, CPR,* 2020 available at:

https://www.cpradr.org/resource-center/protocols-guidelines/model-procedure-order-remote-video-arbitration-proceedings.

[27] Chartered Institute of Arbitrators, *Guidance Note on Remote Dispute Resolution Proceedings,* 2020, available at: https://www.ciarb.org/media/9013/remote-hearings-guidance-note_final_140420.pdf.

[28] Principle 6 read with Schedule B, International Council for Commercial Arbitration, New York City Bar Association, and International Institute for Conflict Prevention and Resolution (CPR), *Protocol on Cyber security in International Arbitration, 2020,* available at:https://cdn.arbitration-icca.org/s3fs-public/document/media_document/icca-nyc_bar-cpr_cybersecurity_protocol_for_international_arbitration_-_print_version.pdf

[29] Indian Arbitration Forum, *IAF Protocol on Virtual Hearings for Arbitrations,* 2020, available at: https://indianarbitrationforum.com/wp-content/themes/iaf/assets/IAF-Protocol-on-Virtual-Hearings-for-Arbitrations-Oct-2020.pdf

9 798890 023872

Printed by Libri Plureos GmbH in Hamburg, Germany